HISTORY'S MYSTERIES

CURIOUS CLUES, COLD CASES, AND PUZZLES FROM THE PAST

KITSON JAZYNKA

NATIONAL GEOGRAPHIC

WASHINGTON, D.C.

CONTENTS

Archaeologists investigate the excavation site of the famous Dead Sea Scrolls, ancient writings discovered more than 60 years ago in a cave in Israel and estimated to be 2,000 years old (see page 134). Top left: Searching for the fugitive D. B. Cooper. Top right: Sponge divers discover the world's first computer.

INTRODUCTION

WHETHER YOU'RE TAKING A PEEK OUTSIDE the bus window as you head to school, or staring down at Earth from a plane 25,000 feet (7,620 m) in the air, you probably already know that our world is a pretty awesome place: It's been around for billions of years. It's beautiful. It's colorful. It's full of surprises. And it's big—really big! In fact, our world is so vast that there are still many places yet to explore—secret spots to be discovered, buried treasures yet to be unearthed, and sunken ships that hold clues to our past. Although we haven't even come close to solving all of the world's mysteries (not to mention mysteries we don't even know about yet!), we investigate. Like detectives, we sort through clues to figure out as much as we can. And who knows, maybe you'll be the next famous archaeologist to discover a treasure.

So ... what are you waiting for? The world is waiting for answers. These mysteries aren't going to solve themselves!

ATLANTIS

STONEHENGE

We can't travel back in time, but artifacts like these bones of a *Coelophysis* dinosaur, ancient rock formations, and statues give us captivating clues about how people and animals lived, long before our time.

MAYA VILLAGE LIFE

1

VANISHED
CIVILIZATIONS

Archaeologists in **CHINA**
once unearthed a 4,000-year-old
BOWL OF
NOODLES.

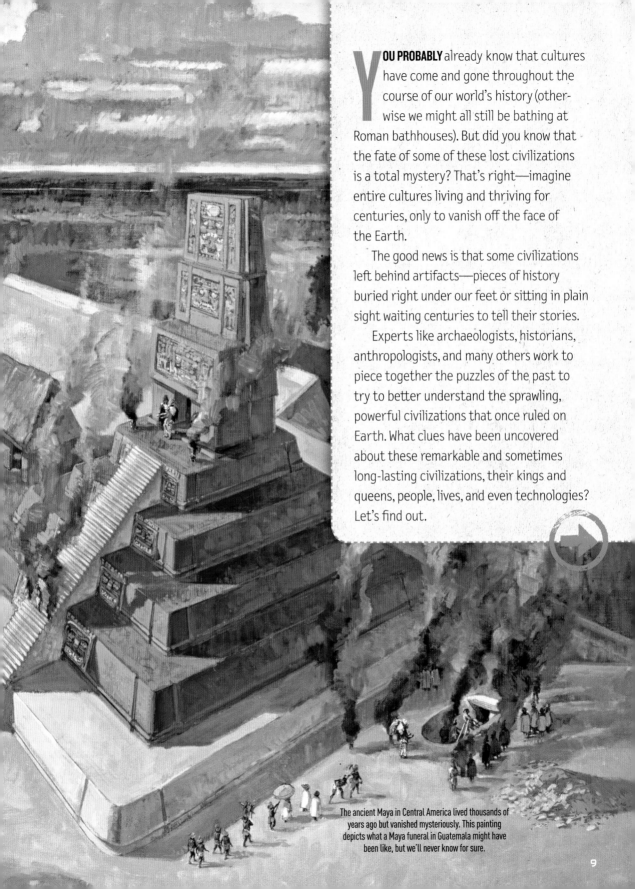

YOU PROBABLY already know that cultures have come and gone throughout the course of our world's history (otherwise we might all still be bathing at Roman bathhouses). But did you know that the fate of some of these lost civilizations is a total mystery? That's right—imagine entire cultures living and thriving for centuries, only to vanish off the face of the Earth.

The good news is that some civilizations left behind artifacts—pieces of history buried right under our feet or sitting in plain sight waiting centuries to tell their stories.

Experts like archaeologists, historians, anthropologists, and many others work to piece together the puzzles of the past to try to better understand the sprawling, powerful civilizations that once ruled on Earth. What clues have been uncovered about these remarkable and sometimes long-lasting civilizations, their kings and queens, people, lives, and even technologies? Let's find out.

The ancient Maya in Central America lived thousands of years ago but vanished mysteriously. This painting depicts what a Maya funeral in Guatemala might have been like, but we'll never know for sure.

THE CIVILIZATION THAT WENT THE WAY OF THE DINOSAURS

MAYA WRITING

"PITZ" STONE HOOP

In the Maya game called "PITZ," players bounced a RUBBER BALL through stone hoops without using their hands.

THE BACKGROUND

THE ANCIENT MAYA flourished in the Central American rain forest about 3,500 years ago. Their civilization was centuries before its time. They had vast cities, grand stone temples, and advances in writing, astronomy, and mathematics. The Maya were even responsible for discovering the concept of zero! In its heyday, the civilization had dozens of cities, stretching across the areas of modern-day Guatemala, Belize, El Salvador, Honduras, and Mexico.

Strangely, about 2,400 years ago, the Maya people vanished, leaving their giant stone pyramids eerily abandoned in the jungle. How could such a sophisticated society just disappear? And what happened to them? To this day, nobody knows for sure.

NORTH AMERICA
ATLANTIC OCEAN
PACIFIC OCEAN
SOUTH AMERICA

Maya Civilization
Gulf of Mexico
Caribbean Sea
MEXICO
BELIZE
GUATEMALA
HONDURAS
PACIFIC OCEAN
EL SALVADOR

THE DETAILS

ARCHAEOLOGISTS DIG, chisel, sweep, and ponder artifacts left behind—from piles of stone to ruins of entire cities and palaces. The Maya were known for having a sophisticated written language, spectacular art, amazing architecture, and complex mathematical and astronomical systems, which is evident from treasures unearthed from the time when they thrived. Their civilization also developed advanced agriculture techniques such as irrigation, composting, and terracing. Historians have pieced together a history of people rich in knowledge and resources. So, if their cities and temples stood the test of time, why didn't they?

MAYA ARCHAEOLOGICAL SITE IN YUCATÁN STATE, MEXICO

THE CLUES

Over the past few decades, archaeologists have discovered hidden ruins that shed light on the destruction of individual Maya villages. And even more recently, they've used advanced technology to study the world at the time when the Maya lived—and perhaps uncover what happened to them. These three clues stand out as possible indicators of what went wrong:

▶ **BURIED IN ASH** In 1978, archaeologists first set eyes on Ceren, a lost village in El Salvador that was accidentally discovered by construction workers. They dug through 16 feet (5 m) of volcanic ash before hitting the roof of a preserved thatched Maya house.

▶ **ALL DRIED UP** In 2009, scientists studying environmental conditions in Mexico's Yucatán Peninsula discovered there had been a sharp reduction in rainfall in the areas where the Maya lived at about the same time their numbers started to dwindle.

▶ **CROP COLLAPSE** NASA conducted computer simulations and collected data that indicate that there was serious deforestation during the time of the Maya—meaning the Maya people cut down a huge amount of trees. This could have effected local climate, caused erosion, and depleted the soil of its nutrients.

DEFORESTATION MIGHT HAVE CONTRIBUTED TO THE DOWNFALL OF THE MAYA.

MAYA STONE CARVING

JAGUAR PAW TEMPLE
IN GUATEMALA

THE THEORIES

THE QUESTION OF WHAT HAPPENED to the Maya has fascinated researchers and the public since 19th-century explorers began discovering these imposing lost cities in the jungles of Central America.

Some evidence, like the volcanic ash discovered at Ceren, suggests a sudden catastrophe, like a mega-earthquake, hurricane, or volcanic eruption, led to the end of the Maya.

But what about those civilizations with ruins still standing?

Some researchers believe that the collapse of the Maya civilization could have been due to a mysterious disease that wiped out the population over a period of about 200 years. Without modern medicine, disease could have spread easily from person to person in a dense city environment. However, many experts now believe the answer isn't so simple. They think it was a combination of factors, such as overpopulation, environmental damage, famine, and drought that may have caused people to abandon their cities slowly over time. Scarce resources, like water and food, also might have caused the system to crumble and led to catastrophic violence and wars with nearby civilizations.

Millions of people in Guatemala today are direct ancestors of the ancient Maya. Many of them still use an ancient Maya dialect as their first language. If only they could spill the secrets of what happened to this fascinating civilization.

WHAT IS UNDER THESE PILES OF DIRT?

One of Cahokia's mounds—called **MONKS MOUND**—is 10 stories high and larger at its base than Egypt's **LARGEST PYRAMID,** or about the same size as **10 FOOTBALL FIELDS.**

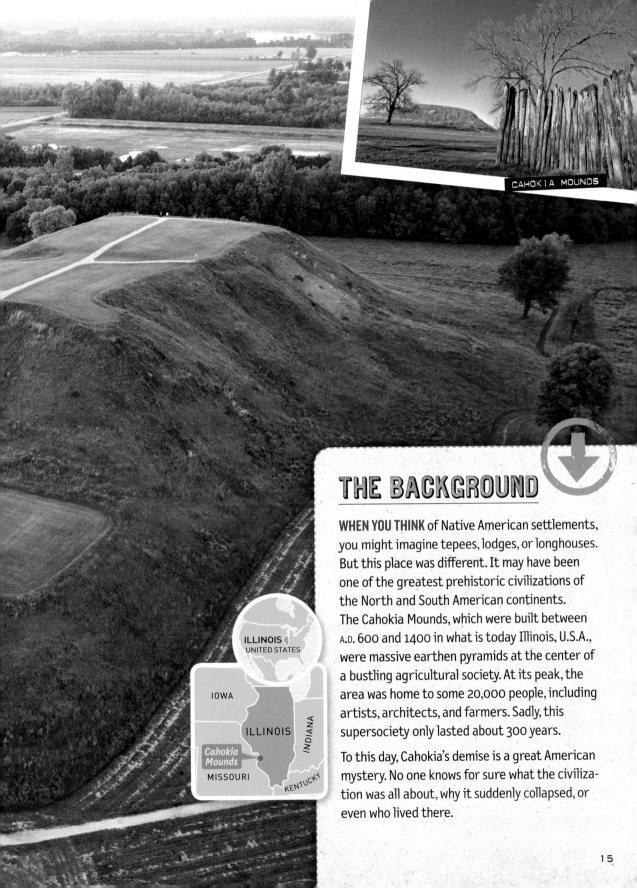

CAHOKIA MOUNDS

THE BACKGROUND

WHEN YOU THINK of Native American settlements, you might imagine tepees, lodges, or longhouses. But this place was different. It may have been one of the greatest prehistoric civilizations of the North and South American continents. The Cahokia Mounds, which were built between A.D. 600 and 1400 in what is today Illinois, U.S.A., were massive earthen pyramids at the center of a bustling agricultural society. At its peak, the area was home to some 20,000 people, including artists, architects, and farmers. Sadly, this supersociety only lasted about 300 years.

To this day, Cahokia's demise is a great American mystery. No one knows for sure what the civilization was all about, why it suddenly collapsed, or even who lived there.

ILLINOIS
UNITED STATES

IOWA

ILLINOIS

INDIANA

Cahokia Mounds

MISSOURI

KENTUCKY

15

THE DETAILS

TODAY, Cahokia's 4,000 acres (1,619 ha) add up to be the largest archaeological site in the United States. Excavations of the Cahokia Mounds have revealed remains of extensive roads and walls. Communities were often arranged around courtyards with large storage pits (probably used to store surplus corn). At six miles (9.7 km) across and with a huge plaza in the center, the city would have rivaled the size of Washington, D.C. It had endless numbers of homes and even its very own wooden Stonehenge-like structure (called "Woodhenge" today), which was made from sacred cedarwood and likely used as a calendar. Cahokia's marvelous, massive, and mysterious mounds give us some insight into how Native Americans lived in North America long before Europeans arrived.

THE CLUES

For decades, researchers have speculated about how Cahokia was planned and built and what it meant to the people who moved into the area 12,000 years ago. We're still learning the secrets of this once magnificent place. Here is what has been discovered so far:

▶ **REMARKABLE RELICS** In 2012, excavation related to the construction of a bridge across the Mississippi River revealed relics (objects that have survived from the past) from what might have been a neighborhood on the outskirts of Cahokia, including the remains of prehistoric homes, a small clay figure of a kneeling woman, and many different types of arrowheads and shells used for trading.

▶ **A CORNY DIET** Archaeological digs have revealed that the Cahokian diet was based on maize, or corn. In addition to the sweet, starchy stuff, they grew sustainable seed-bearing crops like squash and sunflowers.

▶ **KEEP OUT** Between 1175 and 1275, Cahokia's inhabitants built a wall with guard towers and barriers that encircled the main part of the city and was as big as two miles (3.2 km) around.

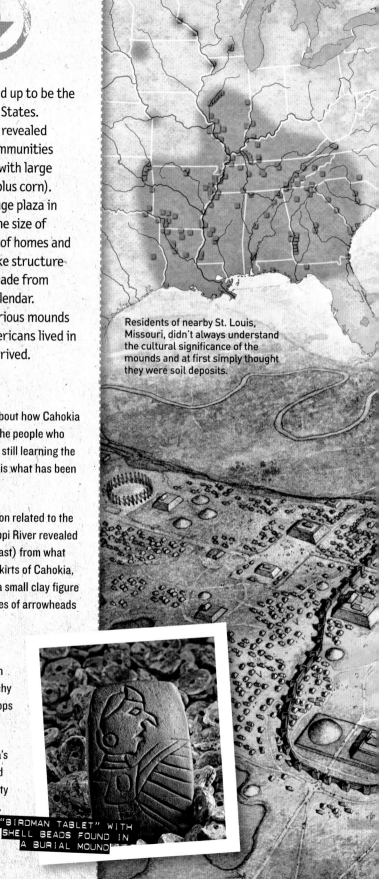

Residents of nearby St. Louis, Missouri, didn't always understand the cultural significance of the mounds and at first simply thought they were soil deposits.

"BIRDMAN TABLET" WITH SHELL BEADS FOUND IN A BURIAL MOUND

ARCHAEOLOGICAL DIG AT CAHOKIA'S MONKS MOUND

THE THEORIES

SIGNS OF DEFENSIVE STRUCTURES like stockades, walls, and guard towers have some archaeologists speculating that conflict might have been the beginning of the end for this once thriving culture. The people who lived here seem to have been trying to protect themselves from somebody. Other archaeologists believe Cahokia was plagued with problems, like disease and famine, from the start. The city may have grown to prominence during an especially favorable climate phase and then shrank when the climate became cooler, drier, and less predictable—wreaking havoc on agriculture and the corn crops people depended on to survive. Perhaps Cahokians migrated beyond the main settlement, as the discovery of relics outside the city suggests, to find better places to live and farm along the Mississippi River. Experts are still digging up clues on this one.

TRUE OR FALSE?

DID THIS CITY REALLY EXIST?

The Earth today has
ABOUT 1,500
active volcanoes, not counting the
ones on the
OCEAN FLOOR.

The caldera (a large volcanic crater formed after an eruption) on the Greek island of Santorini, as seen today. About 3,500 years ago it was the site of the single most powerful explosive event ever witnessed. A new volcano is forming in the crater.

The wealthy empire known as Atlantis might have sunk into the sea after a massive volcano.

THE BACKGROUND

THE GREAT GREEK PHILOSOPHER Plato created the legend of the powerful city of Atlantis in his writings that tried to explain the universe. In works called *Timaeus* and *Critias*, written about 360 B.C., Plato tells an epic tale of war in which Athens defeats a splendid city called Atlantis. The city was said to sink into the ocean. Plato's accounts of the city were so specific and detailed that many believe it was a real place. People have searched down to the seafloor and back again to try to find evidence that it existed. So far, researchers have come up empty-handed.

Nobody really knows whether this spectacular submerged city actually ever existed, but it's a mesmerizing mystery. Is there any truth to this legend?

ATLANTIC OCEAN
EUROPE
AFRICA

ITALY
TURKEY
GREECE
Mediterranean Sea
Malta
Santorini
LIBYA
EGYPT

THE DETAILS

PLATO'S WAR STORY includes dozens of details about what Atlantis might have looked like 9,000 years ago. For instance, he mentions concentric circles around the city, the presence of black and red stones, and that it was located near the sea. Still, even the greatest modern scholars can't say for sure whether Plato's Atlantis was fact or fiction.

THE GREEK PHILOSOPHER PLATO

THE CLUES

Possible locations for the lost city of Atlantis have been suggested in each of the world's four oceans, on mainland Europe, and in the Mediterranean Sea. These three clues give us hints at where the real Atlantis might have been, if it existed at all:

▶ **SUBMERGED SECRETS** A team of scientists diving near North Bimini Island in the Bahamas discovered a giant, flat limestone block formation underwater. Its sharp corners and straight lines suggest to scientists that it was man-made.

▶ **ARTSY ARTIFACTS** In the early 1900s, an archaeologist discovered an ancient throne in a trench dug on a hilltop settlement on the Greek island of Crete. Further digs revealed a sophisticated palace filled with 3,000-year-old art like wall hangings and pots.

▶ **SOGGY SITUATION** In 2011, after searching with satellite photography, ground-penetrating radar, and underwater technology, scientists discovered a lost city buried under a marsh in Spain.

RUINS OF AN ANCIENT HOME ON SANTORINI

THE THEORIES

REAL OR IMAGINED, Atlantis is one of the world's most famous places. The traditional explanation of Atlantis, for those who want to believe it was real, is that the city was located near the island of Santorini in the Aegean Sea. The place has a history of volcano eruptions. It was also the site of a once flourishing port city discovered in 1967. This place, called Akrotiri, has a lot of similarities to details of Plato's description of Atlantis, like its proximity to the sea and the presence of black and red stones.

But most scientists doubt that Atlantis actually existed. They think that in Plato's time readers understood his story to be a parable, or a moral lesson, about corruption and greed and that in the Middle Ages, fiction may have morphed into something readers believed was fact. Other theories include that Atlantis was on one of the many Greek islands. Still others say it was in southern Spain or Malta, like the lost city discovered by scientists in 2011, which may have been wiped out by tsunamis, volcanic eruptions, or even a meteor strike. Was this city fact or fiction? We might never know for sure.

THIS MYSTERY'S THE CAT'S MEOW!

CORTÉS'S exploration of the Americas led him to discover the area that would later become California.

THE BACKGROUND

1 **DATING BACK TO THE** 16th century, legends have circulated about a mysterious city buried deep in the unblemished emerald rain forest of eastern Honduras. The Ciudad Blanca, or the White City, was rumored to be a metropolis built of white stone and was also known as the Lost City of the Jaguar.

Indigenous stories referred to a distant white palace where Native Americans took refuge from Spanish conquistadores and worshipped a jaguar-like god. Explorers, prospectors, and early aviators spoke of glimpsing the white ruins, which were first recorded by the Spanish conquistador Hernán Cortés in 1526.

But is this legendary lost jungle city real?

THE DETAILS

2 **IN 1927,** Charles Lindbergh, the famous American aviator, flew over eastern Honduras and

CHARLES LINDBERGH

PARTIALLY BURIED
ARTIFACT

THE LUSH
MOSQUITIA JUNGLE

reported seeing a white city peeking up through the treetops. And that same year, archaeologists documented finding stone objects, including an effigy of a "werejaguar" (a sculpture probably representing a human and spirit animal combination) deep in the jungles of Central America.

THE THEORIES

3 **WHETHER OR NOT** they believe in the Ciudad Blanca, most archaeologists who have studied the area agree that the remote rain forest of eastern Honduras—a vast region of swamps, rivers, mountains, and unexplored places—has many "lost cities." They think that this valley contains the ruins of a real lost city, abandoned for at least half a millennium. But we don't know who lived there and why their civilization didn't survive.

NEW EVIDENCE REVEALED!

In 2015, archaeologists sponsored by the National Geographic Society discovered what could be this legendary city's ruins. The team spent a month recovering artifacts from the "lost white city." They found earthen pyramids, plazas, and a cache of pristine stone artifacts—including ceremonial seats, a statue of a bird wearing something like a helmet, and finely carved vessels decorated with snakes. They are believed to date back to A.D. 1000 to 1400. The objects, according to lead archaeologist Chris Fisher (see page 152 for an interview with him!), may have been a powerful ritual display. Scientists are still gathering clues, trying to piece together who lived there, what happened to them, and if there are more "lost cities" still to be discovered in that area.

UNEXPLAINED DEATHS & DISAPPEARANCES

Amelia Earhart, the first woman to fly solo across the Atlantic Ocean in 1932, was a fearless pioneer for women and aviation. In 1937, she tried to circumnavigate (fly all the way around) the globe and mysteriously vanished without a trace somewhere over the Pacific Ocean. To this day, despite numerous search efforts, nobody knows for sure what happened to her.

WHEN A WHOLE civilization disappears, the world pays attention. But what if just one person, a crowd, or random people vanish suddenly, under eerily similar circumstances? Well, that might fly under the radar a bit longer, if we didn't love a good mystery so much. When something—or someone—goes missing and there's no reasonable explanation, history buffs grapple with the truth. Was it something sinister? Perhaps foul play? Or is there a perfectly innocent explanation? Detectives wrestle with timelines, dusty artifacts, even eyewitness accounts. But are they reliable? Are we linking evidence when there's actually no connection? Sometimes clues are subject to interpretation, but let's see what you make of these age-old cases.

THIS MYSTERY HAS BEEN ON ONE LONG FLIGHT.

AMELIA WITH
PRESIDENT HOOVER

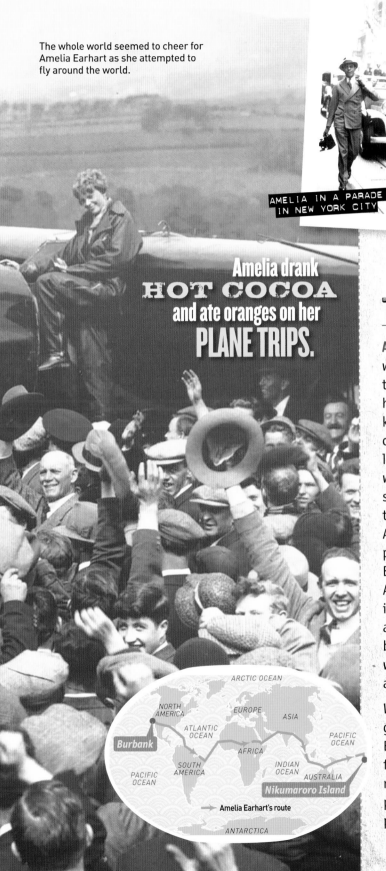

The whole world seemed to cheer for Amelia Earhart as she attempted to fly around the world.

AMELIA IN A PARADE IN NEW YORK CITY

Amelia drank **HOT COCOA** and ate oranges on her **PLANE TRIPS.**

ARCTIC OCEAN

NORTH AMERICA

EUROPE

ASIA

ATLANTIC OCEAN

PACIFIC OCEAN

Burbank

AFRICA

PACIFIC OCEAN

SOUTH AMERICA

INDIAN OCEAN

AUSTRALIA

Nikumaroro Island

→ Amelia Earhart's route

ANTARCTICA

THE BACKGROUND

AMELIA EARHART was just five years old when the Wright brothers invented the airplane. When her father took her to an air show at age 23, she knew she was destined to soar in the clouds. She saved money for flying lessons and became one of the first women to be a pilot. Then she set her sights even higher. She wanted to be the first woman pilot to cross the Atlantic Ocean (even though many people had died trying), and in 1932, Earhart made the long, hard trip. Afterward, she wrote books and gave interviews and speeches about her adventure. Next, she dreamed even bigger—she wanted to fly around the world. She got a bigger, faster plane and took off to make history.

What happened next was one of the greatest mysteries of all time: Earhart was never seen or heard from again. No one has ever determined what happened to the young pilot and her navigator, although people have lots of theories!

THE DETAILS

ON A BRIGHT, spring day in May 1937, Amelia Earhart and her navigator, Fred Noonan, took off from what is now known as the Bob Hope Airport in Burbank in California to fly around the world. Their flight path led them over deserts and mountains in the western U.S., south to Florida and then across the Atlantic Ocean. After crossing Africa and Asia, they made a pit stop in July on a tiny, hard-to-find island in the southwest Pacific Ocean called New Guinea. Then they took off with 2,556 miles (4,113 km) to go before the next stop. They were never heard from again. But was that the end? In the years since, researchers have found evidence of human life on a tiny island in the Pacific. From a jar of freckle cream to human remains. Could Earhart have made this place her home?

THE CLUES

Eighty years after this adventurous pilot's final stop, the mystery of Amelia Earhart's disappearance still has altitude. What happened to this brave young pilot and her experienced navigator? These clues might help bring this mystery down to earth:

▶ **CALL FOR HELP** Earhart is said to have disappeared on July 2, 1937, but researchers have documented about 100 distress calls from her plane between July 2 and July 6 of that year, indicating that her plane may have been operating after July 2.

▶ **IN PLANE VIEW** In 2013, researchers released sonar images of what they believed to be pieces of Earhart's small plane, 660 feet (201 m) underwater off the island of Nikumaroro.

▶ **CASTAWAY** In 1940, bones from a female human skeleton were found on the island of Nikumaroro, in the western Pacific Ocean. In 2012, a group of researchers found pieces of a small cosmetic jar nearly identical to a popular face cream used to get rid of freckles (Earhart had freckles!), along with a piece of a woman's shoe and a pocket knife similar to one Earhart was said to have had.

PLANNING WITH HER COPILOT

AMELIA AND FRED OVER THE GOLDEN GATE BRIDGE IN 1937

THE THEORIES

A MASSIVE RESCUE EFFORT searched unsuccessfully for Earhart, and the search for clues continues to this day. At the time of her disappearance, most people believed she died when her airplane ran out of gas and crashed in the Pacific. Others believed she may have been captured by the Japanese in those years leading up to World War II. Experts believe Earhart made changes to the airplane's radio that may have limited her ability to communicate, which could have led to a crash. In 2016, aviation researchers and forensic anthropologists studying the bones found on Nikumaroro reported that they believed they were Earhart's remains. If those bones are indeed hers, that suggests she died as a castaway on the island after some kind of crash landing. But without living relatives to compare DNA samples to the remains, we may never know for sure what happened to this fearless pilot.

Amelia once said, "I believe that women have as much courage as men." She was the first president of the Ninety-Nines, a group of women pilots.

MONSTER
MANHUNT
LASTS FOR MORE THAN
400 YEARS.

THE BACKGROUND

IT'S A MYSTERY that has intrigued Americans for centuries: What happened to the 100 or so lost colonists of North Carolina's Roanoke Island? They arrived and settled in 1587 near what is today Manteo, North Carolina, U.S.A. Not long after, the colony's governor, John White, left the colonists so he could return to England for supplies. When White arrived back on the shores of the New World in 1590, he was shocked and dismayed to find only a startling silence and an eerily empty shell of a village.

Great efforts to solve this great North American disappearing act have produced dozens of theories but no clear answers. But these colonists did leave behind some tantalizing clues ...

ART SHOWING JOHN WHITE RETURNING TO THE ABANDONED SETTLEMENT

Some archaeologists believe **AMERICAN INDIANS** have lived in what today is Virginia, U.S.A., for at least **1,600 YEARS.**

REPLICA OF A 16TH-CENTURY SHIP, LIKE THE ONES COLONISTS WOULD HAVE USED

UNITED STATES
NORTH CAROLINA

WEST VIRGINIA
KY. VIRGINIA
Roanoke Island
TENN. NORTH CAROLINA
GEORGIA SOUTH CAROLINA
ATLANTIC OCEAN

THE DETAILS

←

THE COLOR ENGRAVING SHOWS HOW VILLAGE LIFE MIGHT HAVE BEEN IN THE INDIAN TOWN OF SECOTAN, VIRGINIA.

THE LOST COLONISTS included entire families—a total of 17 women, 11 children, and 90 men. Today's technologically advanced searches have harnessed the power of magnetometers, ground-penetrating radar, and satellite surveys, but so far they haven't yielded much new evidence about what happened to the stray settlers.

THE CLUES

What could possibly have happened to make an entire colony of people disappear? Where did they go and why? Archaeologists and historians have been searching for these missing persons for centuries. Here are some clues they've uncovered:

▶ **TEXT MESSAGES** The word "Croatoan" was carved into a fort's gatepost and "Cro" was etched into a nearby tree. At the time, Hatteras Island—50 miles (80 km) southeast of the colonists' original location—was known as Croatoan Island.

▶ **ON THE MOVE** Archaeologists have found European objects, including a sword hilt, broken English bowls, and a fragment of a slate writing tablet, among a nearby Native American settlement called Mettaquem.

▶ **MODERN TECHNOLOGY** Recent discoveries by scientists have also included buried iron cannons, graves, and coffins—that may date back to the time of the colonists—in the area where Mettaquem would have been located.

Trinety ha

Hatorasck

A 16TH-CENTURY MAP DEPICTING THE COLONY OF ROANOKE ON THE COAST OF PRESENT-DAY NORTH CAROLINA. WHAT HAPPENED TO THE SETTLERS THERE REMAINS ONE OF AMERICA'S OLDEST UNSOLVED MYSTERIES.

THE THEORIES

THEORIES ABOUT THE DISAPPEARANCE of the colonists have ranged from an annihilating disease to a violent rampage by local Native American tribes. Tensions had already been brewing between local tribes and two previous groups of colonists. The fact that the colonists brought women and children meant that they were clearly planning to stay. The Secotan people who controlled much of the land and the Chowanoke who controlled the nearby waterways might have been angered that the colonists were depleting them of their land and resources.

One theory is that the colonists, facing limited supplies, disease, and threats from Native American neighbors, split up into smaller groups and dispersed.

Some historians believe that the displaced colonists may not have survived for long wherever they went. But according to other accounts, a local chief named Powhatan had made plans to wipe out the remaining colonists. Artifacts found at the Native American town Mettaquem suggest some of the lost colonists may have sought refuge there, but we'll never know if they were fleeing from famine, disease, an attack, or all of those awful things.

ARTIFACT FOUND
AT ROANOKE

33

THEY SHIPPED OUT,
BUT WHERE
DID THEY
GO?

THE BACKGROUND

IN DECEMBER 1872, the American cargo ship *Mary Celeste* bobbed on the waves on a clear, sunny day near the Azores (a series of volcanic islands near Portugal) in the Atlantic Ocean. The traditional two-masted sailing ship, called a brigantine, was fully stocked. Personal items sat undisturbed. Its instruments were working, and the ship was full of cargo. There was just one problem: Not a single one of the 10 people who should have been on board—a crew of seven, plus the captain and his wife and child—could be found.

More than 150 years after the *Mary Celeste* was found sailing solo, the fate of the people on board remains one of history's greatest maritime mysteries. Sail on to the next page for clues!

THE DETAILS

A MONTH BEFORE the *Mary Celeste* was found, the ship left New York and sailed for Italy. But something went awfully awry. Fast forward to that day near the Azores when the captain of a passing ship, the *Dei Gratia*, noticed the *Mary Celeste* bobbing erratically and stopped to investigate. By that time, the *Mary Celeste* was floating some 600 miles (965 km) off the coast of Portugal. A search party boarded the boat looking for answers but found it deserted. They found no sign of distress and no hint of foul play. But they were in the middle of the ocean, so where did everybody go?

THE CLUES

When it was found, the sails of the *Mary Celeste* were still up. There was little or no structural damage to the vessel. No trace of a survivor of the *Mary Celeste* has ever been found. Here are a few clues that might help us figure out—or at least imagine—what might have happened to that ill-fated ship:

▶ **A MISSING LIFEBOAT** The search party found a single missing lifeboat and a frayed rope trailing behind the ship.

▶ **A SINKING FEELING** When found, the bottom of the *Mary Celeste* sloshed with three feet (1 m) of water. A disassembled pump was discovered, too.

▶ **AN EXPLOSIVE CLUE** The search party found some 1,700 barrels of a flammable substance called ethanol on board the ship.

An estimated **THREE MILLION** vessels—from Phoenician merchant ships to Japanese submarines— have been **LOST AT SEA.**

THE THEORIES

OVER THE YEARS, historians and other experts have scrutinized the ship's log, studied weather patterns, and pored over maps to figure out what could have happened to the people on board the *Mary Celeste*. Could it have been an attack by pirates, or a mutiny? A run-in with a monster from the depths? Were the humans on board made ill by something? Many theories have floated around, even one that an evil spell was to blame for bad things happening to the ship's 12 different owners!

One researcher found records documenting that the *Mary Celeste* had carried coal in a previous voyage. They say that the coal dust and debris from the previous voyage could have clogged the ship's pump, making it hard to pump water out of the ship during a bad storm. Another theory suggested a fire broke out on board, forcing everybody to flee into the lifeboat. But without evidence of scorched damage within the ship, that idea didn't hold much water—until 2006, when a scientist did an experiment to see if the fumes from the ethanol could have caused a contained explosion. He made a model of the ship and set the fumes alight, which caused an impressive bang and flames, but nothing actually caught fire. Experts now think it's possible the fumes from the ethanol could have combusted, causing the alarmed captain to hurry everyone into a lifeboat. During that time, a storm may have hit. Although the large, sturdy *Mary Celeste* could survive the storm, the tiny lifeboat and its occupants might have vanished into the sea, leaving behind a single, frayed piece of rope.

CREW OVERBOARD!

THE ONLY THING WE DO KNOW ABOUT THIS GUY IS THAT HIS NAME WASN'T D. B. COOPER.

THE BACKGROUND

IN NOVEMBER 1971, a man executed an incredible crime that still has law enforcement officials scratching their heads. Going by the name D.B. Cooper, a man boarded a plane, flying from Portland, Oregon, to Seattle, Washington, U.S.A. After takeoff, the guy took control of the plane by telling flight attendants that his briefcase had an explosive in it. He demanded $200,000 and four parachutes. He allowed the pilot to land the aircraft in Seattle, drop passengers off, get D.B. his money, and take flight again as Cooper demanded. Cooper then instructed the pilot to fly the plane toward Mexico at a low altitude. But somewhere over the forests of the Pacific Northwest, the dastardly daredevil opened the plane's rear stairs and jumped, wearing a dark business suit and two parachutes, into the ink-black night, never to be seen again.

Who was D.B. Cooper? Did he survive? Where did he end up? These are questions that criminal investigators have asked themselves for 45 years without luck. What do you make of this enigmatic escape artist?

Cascade mountains in Washington State, U.S.A. Carrying $200,000 and wearing a business suit, D. B. Cooper parachuted from a low-flying plane over a forest in the Pacific northwest region of the U.S. during an epic getaway, part of a crime that has never been solved.

FBI AGENTS WORKING ON SOLVING THE CASE

FBI SKETCHES OF D.B. COOPER

THE DETAILS

UNFORTUNATELY, as with a lot of cold cases, there's very little evidence to suggest who D.B. Cooper really was or what happened to him. Back in the 1970s, law enforcement didn't have access to some of the high-powered research technology available today. But they did investigate more than 800 suspects within five years of the crime. After many more years of hard work and little progress in their investigation, the U.S. Federal Bureau of Investigation officially closed the case of D.B. Cooper in 2016.

THE CLUES

Even though investigators closed the case, the identity, motives, and locations of D.B. Cooper are still unsolved. The crafty criminal in this intriguing case left very few clues for investigators to follow.

▶ **RUSHING OFF** A black, clip-on tie was discovered on D. B.'s airplane seat. Investigators think that in his rush to get off the plane, he may have left it behind. It may not have seemed like much of a clue at the time, but particular particles found on the tie, including traces of titanium, aluminum, and stainless steel, were like forensic gold to investigators.

▶ **MONEY TRAIL** In 1980, a boy found $5,800 of Cooper's ransom money in a bundle of $20 bills on a sandbar in the Columbia River near Portland, Oregon. This led some to believe that while his money survived the fall, he did not—or else he wouldn't have left any money behind.

▶ **THE GROCER GOES MISSING** Two years before Cooper's death-defying robbery, a grocery store manager named Robert Richard Lepsy went missing, leaving behind a family. In 2015, his daughter, Lisa Lepsy, produced a photo of her father. She believed her father assumed D. B. Cooper's fake identity. The resemblance was striking.

FBI AGENTS SEARCH FOR COOPER'S RANSOM MONEY IN 1980.

On November 25, 1971, the hijacked jet airliner prepares for refueling on the runway.

THE THEORIES

MOST PEOPLE BELIEVE D.B. Cooper may not even have survived the jump out of the airplane. Operating and steering a parachute isn't easy, and he would have landed in a wooded area at night. All those trees could have affected his ability to land safely. In 2016, a group of citizen researchers homed in on theories that he possibly worked in a manufacturing plant that made aircraft because of the unique combination of elements found on the tie authorities found. Unfortunately, without finding new evidence, or the man himself, his identity will remain a mystery. Since the case has been closed, we may never know for sure who this man was or what fueled his desire to steal all that money and jump out of a plane with it.

RANSOM MONEY FOUND BY A BOY ON A SANDBAR NEAR PORTLAND, OREGON

41

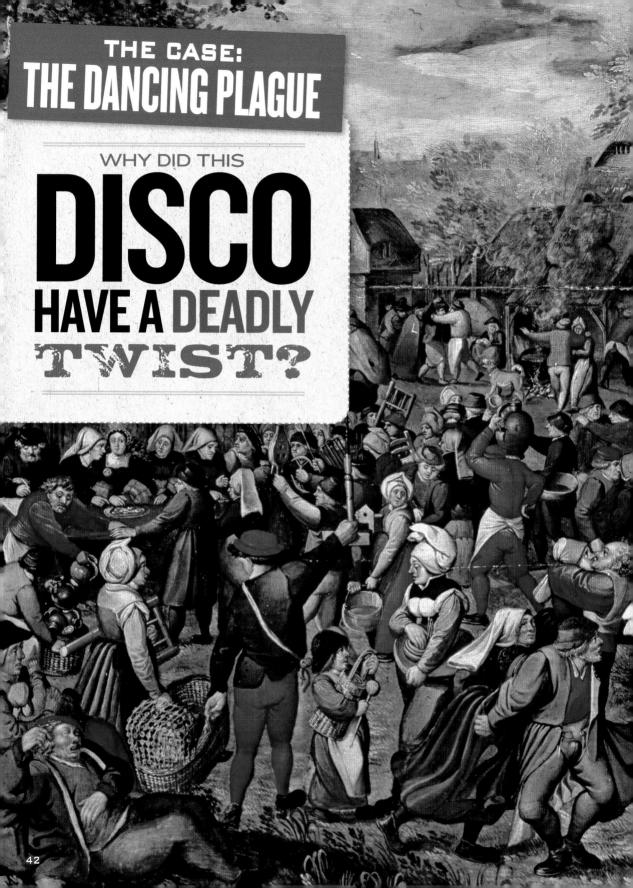

WHY DID THIS

DISCO

HAVE A DEADLY

TWIST?

Although the bizarre dancing frenzy might have looked like this village festival scene, it was certainly nothing to celebrate.

ATLANTIC OCEAN · **EUROPE** · **FRANCE** · **AFRICA**

UNITED KINGDOM · BELGIUM · LUX. · GERMANY · **Strasbourg** · SWITZ. · **FRANCE** · ITALY · ATLANTIC OCEAN · SPAIN · Mediterranean Sea

THE BACKGROUND

WHEN A WOMAN NAMED Frau Troffea danced a lively jig in the streets of Strasbourg, France, in 1518, people around cheered her lively sense of fun. Frau Troffea didn't seem to mind there was no music playing. But when she danced day and night for six days without stopping, people grew concerned. Even more concerning, others soon joined her. After a month, some 400 people were dancing in the streets without stopping. Authorities figured the dancers would just wear themselves out and have the good sense to stop. They even built a giant stage for the dancers! But at the peak of this perplexing plague, about 15 people a day were dying from heart attacks or just plain old exhaustion.

These frenzied folks danced themselves to death, but why? The mystery has lingered for centuries: What caused this horrific and deadly compulsion to dance? Hustle over to the next page for some theories …

THE DETAILS

BEFORE 1518, smaller "dancing epidemics" had been documented in France and in the areas known today as Belgium and Luxembourg. In Strasbourg that summer, the city was forced to cart the dead out of the city by the wagonload. In a trancelike state, dancers cried for help but couldn't seem to stop. At the time, doctors reported that the illness was caused by "hot blood." Suddenly in September, the madness—which was documented by doctors, writers, and priests—stopped. The deadly dance claimed 400 victims in all. People involved in the dancing plague didn't seem in control of their movements and, by many accounts, didn't even seem conscious. Were they acting by choice, or were they under the influence of a darker power?

THE CLUES

For such an old mystery, the event is well documented. But detailed descriptions of the dancers' state and their response to treatment efforts are sparse. The clues only seem to confirm that the people were not dancing out of their own free will.

▶ **TURN UP THE MUSIC** In an attempt to control the dancers, the local government set up a stage and musicians to play. But it didn't calm people down. Instead, it amped up the dancing to new levels of hysteria.

▶ **TRANCE DANCE** Dancers appeared to lose control of their actions, or to be in a trance. They seemed to be in a state in which they were unaware of their bloodied feet and aching arms.

▶ **WHEN IT'S OVER, IT'S OVER** The dancing stopped as suddenly as it started. Those who survived the terrible dance-a-thon ceased their dancing and resumed their normal lives.

AN ARTIST'S DEPICTION OF DANCING EPIDEMIC VICTIMS

Strasbourg, France, where the deadly dancing epidemic swept through in the summer of 1518

A PRIEST TRYING TO HELP VICTIMS

THE THEORIES

RESEARCHERS, historians, and doctors from that time speculated the spasms and erratic dancing were caused by anything from demonic possession to widespread psychological illness due to famine. Today, some scientists think these "dancers" may have ingested a common grain mold called ergot that attacks the central nervous system and causes violent spasms, convulsions, and a crawling feeling on the skin. But without more recent evidence and epidemics to examine, it's hard to know for sure.

WAS THIS YOUNG ROYAL HIDDEN OR TRAGICALLY KILLED?

AS A GIRL, cheerful Anastasia (called Nastya by her family) wove flowers into her hair and had a little dog named Shvibzik (sounds like sha-VEE-zic).

THE BACKGROUND

1 **THE YOUNGEST DAUGHTER** of Russia's royal family at the time, Anastasia was born in 1901 and grew up in a palace with her family, surrounded by her siblings and pets. But when World War I started, things changed. Her father's life was in danger. The people of Russia were incredibly unhappy and started a revolution. When Anastasia was 17, revolutionaries stormed the palace and imprisoned and then murdered the royal family. Although the remains of her family were discovered, for many years those of Anastasia and her brother, Alexei, were never found.

Stories swirled about what happened to Anastasia, followed by books and even movies about the legendary princess who some believed may have embarked on a secret life.

THE DETAILS

2 **IN 1918,** the murder of the royal family made headlines all over the world. Rumors ran rampant that Anastasia, and perhaps her brother, had miraculously and mysteriously survived the deadly attack on her family. To further fuel this speculation, in 1991 a forensic study identified the bodies of Anastasia's family members and servants, but as some people had thought, the bodies of the princess and her brother were not with the group. More than 30 women in Russia and as far away as the United States claimed to be the lost princess. None of them turned out to be real royals.

THE THEORIES

3 **FOR MANY YEARS,** most historians believed that Anastasia and her brother, for reasons nobody knows, were simply buried elsewhere. Others said the family

ROYAL FAMILY Anastasia (third from the right) poses with her family, including her father, Tsar Nicholas II of Russia; her mother, Tsarina Alexandra Feodorovna; her sisters Olga, Maria, and Tatiana; and her younger brother, Alexei.

jewels were sewn into the siblings' clothing for safekeeping and acted as shields to protect Anastasia and her brother from bullets. Could the princess have escaped? The question of whether or not Anastasia survived was one of the most talked-about mysteries of the time.

NEW EVIDENCE REVEALED!

SIBERIAN FOREST

In 2007, forensic scientists identified bodies found in a shallow grave in a snowy Siberian forest as Anastasia and Alexei. But why their bodies were buried separately from their family remains a mystery.

3

CREATURES
OF MYTH
AND LEGEND

HAVE YOU EVER MET A CRYPTID? A creature of legend, maybe with slimy scales, jagged teeth, and a killer reputation? Even if you've never seen one, or aren't totally sure that they exist, the mere thought of these mysterious shadowy monsters gives us the chills.

Few scientific facts have ever surfaced to confirm the existence of these scary beasts. Some scientists say that claiming to have seen mysterious creatures is just human nature. We seem to want to find meaning in the strange things we see, hear, touch, taste, or feel. Read on to find out more about cryptids and other monsters that have kept people sleeping with one eye open for centuries.

KONGAMATO

DON'T ROCK THE BOAT WHEN THIS FLYING MONSTER COMES TO TOWN.

It doesn't matter if you're talking about the wild wetlands of Zambia or the highest heights of the Himalaya, you just never know what kind of curious cryptids you might run into—when you least expect it.

THE BACKGROUND

DEEP IN THE HEART OF AFRICA, in the swamps of Zambia, Angola, and the Congo, there's a legend about a flying monster called the Kongamato, which translates to "breaker of boats." A run-in with the Kongamato is said to be worse than an encounter with a rogue elephant, a man-eating lion, or even a demon. Locals in these areas carry charms for good luck at river crossings and near wetlands, where the creature is said to lurk.

But is there any truth to these local stories? Interestingly, going back about a hundred years ago, explorers and visitors to the region also started reporting encounters with a giant flying creature—and their descriptions were oddly similar. Coincidence? Or is there some truth to this story? What could this crazy creature be?

EUROPE

ASIA

AFRICA

Where
Kongamato
is found

INDIAN
OCEAN

ATLANTIC
OCEAN

THE DETAILS

BEGINNING IN THE EARLY 1900s when there was an influx of explorers from other continents, some visitors to central Africa began reporting run-ins with a giant, flying creature that they described as having a long tail, an enormous wing-span, a narrow head, and very sharp teeth. What they described sounded a lot like a pterosaur, a kind of dinosaur that, by modern scientific theory, should have been extinct. And what's more, when locals in the area were shown a drawing of a pterosaur, they identified it as the Kongamato!

THE CLUES

Reportedly seen soaring over swamps, the Kongamato is said to have leathery wings, a long beak filled with sharp teeth, and a bad habit of swooping down from the sky to smash boats that paddle into its territory. Is this creature real, or just local superstition? Here are three accounts that might lend some credibility to the locals' claims.

▶ **EXPLORER'S EXPOSÉ** In a book that was published in 1923, an explorer described the Kongamato as a real creature. He wrote that the Kongamato lived near rivers and was very dangerous and known to attack boats and even people.

▶ **SPECTACLE IN THE SKY** In 1956, an engineer in Zambia reportedly saw two prehistoric-looking creatures flying slowly and silently directly overhead. He observed their long tails, narrow heads, and wingspans greater than three feet (1 m) across. He also reported seeing rather large pointy teeth.

▶ **CREATURE CLASH** In the 1950s, a man came into a local hospital in central Africa with a severe wound in his chest. He claimed to have had a run-in with a creature deep in the swamps. When he was asked to describe what the creature looked like, he apparently drew a picture that had a striking resemblance to a pterosaur.

SHOEBILL STORK

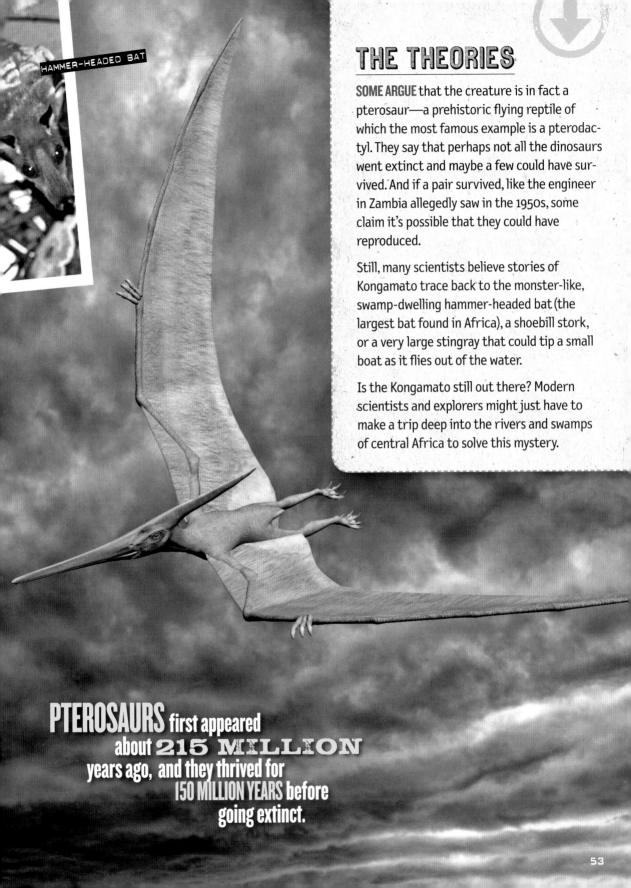

HAMMER-HEADED BAT

THE THEORIES

SOME ARGUE that the creature is in fact a pterosaur—a prehistoric flying reptile of which the most famous example is a pterodactyl. They say that perhaps not all the dinosaurs went extinct and maybe a few could have survived. And if a pair survived, like the engineer in Zambia allegedly saw in the 1950s, some claim it's possible that they could have reproduced.

Still, many scientists believe stories of Kongamato trace back to the monster-like, swamp-dwelling hammer-headed bat (the largest bat found in Africa), a shoebill stork, or a very large stingray that could tip a small boat as it flies out of the water.

Is the Kongamato still out there? Modern scientists and explorers might just have to make a trip deep into the rivers and swamps of central Africa to solve this mystery.

PTEROSAURS first appeared about **215 MILLION** years ago, and they thrived for **150 MILLION YEARS** before going extinct.

IS THIS
HAIRY
BEAST
LOST OR
FOUND?

THE BACKGROUND

THE WORD "YETI" MEANS "little manlike animal" in the Tibetan language. Legendary yetis are known to be hairy (and not so little) ogres that look like human-bear hybrids with jagged fangs and big toes. These mysterious creatures are still reported to be seen today, roaming the icy, desolate, and uninhabitable mountains in Asia's Himalayan mountain range. The big, fur-covered beast is said to steal people at night. The debate has raged for centuries about whether this scary guy is man, myth, or ... bear! Claw your way to the next page and see what conclusions you can draw about this crypt-astic creature.

ASIA
TIBET
INDIAN OCEAN

CHINA
TIBET
HIMALAYA
NEPAL
BHUTAN
INDIA

POSSIBLE YETI FOOTPRINTS

This snowy mountain valley high in the Himalayan mountains in India might make the perfect winter hideout for a yeti and members of his furry family and friends.

THE DETAILS

AS FAR BACK AS THE 16TH CENTURY, Sherpas, a once nomadic people from Tibet, have been spreading stories about this hairy fellow during their travels. According to legend, yetis stand up to seven to eight feet (2 to 2.4 m) tall, weigh up to 400 pounds (181 kg), and love to snack on goats. They've been reported to kill yaks (domesticated wild oxen) the size of buffalo with a single swipe of their massive hands, leaving behind only big-toed footprints. For decades, cryptid enthusiasts, scientists, and lovers of local yore have pursued hard evidence of the existence of the elusive creature.

1976 PHOTO OF A PRESERVED SKULL AND HAND SOME SAY BELONGED TO A YETI!

THE CLUES

So is there any truth to the stories of a heavy-duty hibernator stalking the remote mountain areas of the Himalaya? No matter how you look at this mystery, the facts are bear-y suspicious. Follow these clues like big tracks in the snow to better understand this stomping stumper.

▶ **ROCKY ROAD** In 1986, a man hiking in the Himalaya photographed what he thought was a yeti standing in the snow.

▶ **PROMISING SPECIMENS** Yeti believers have crossed the Himalayan mountains, hiked icy glaciers, searched caves, and tested DNA on samples of promising specimens, like a furry scalp and animal hair. In the 1950s, even Hollywood actor James Stewart bought into the hype and collected what he believed was a yeti finger!

▶ **FOOT-LONG FOOT** Supposed yeti footprints, measuring about 12 inches (30.5 cm) long and five inches (12.7 cm) wide, have been found, but experts believe they're actually animal tracks.

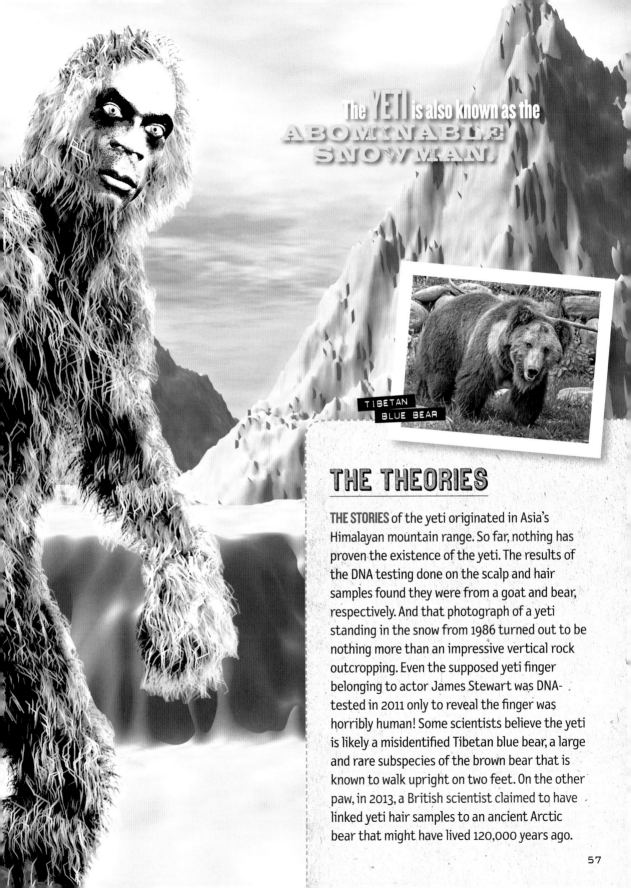

The **YETI** is also known as the **ABOMINABLE SNOWMAN.**

TIBETAN BLUE BEAR

THE THEORIES

THE STORIES of the yeti originated in Asia's Himalayan mountain range. So far, nothing has proven the existence of the yeti. The results of the DNA testing done on the scalp and hair samples found they were from a goat and bear, respectively. And that photograph of a yeti standing in the snow from 1986 turned out to be nothing more than an impressive vertical rock outcropping. Even the supposed yeti finger belonging to actor James Stewart was DNA-tested in 2011 only to reveal the finger was horribly human! Some scientists believe the yeti is likely a misidentified Tibetan blue bear, a large and rare subspecies of the brown bear that is known to walk upright on two feet. On the other paw, in 2013, a British scientist claimed to have linked yeti hair samples to an ancient Arctic bear that might have lived 120,000 years ago.

KRAKEN

IS THIS
JUST A
SCARY
SQUID?

THE BACKGROUND

AS FAR BACK AS the 12th century, tales of huge, tentacled sea monsters have thrilled, chilled, and terrified humans. Norwegian seafarers dubbed these awesome beasts "kraken." By the 18th century, the kraken still had a fearsome reputation and was once described as a "floating island." The sea monster's legendarily long, suction cup–covered tentacles could reach the top of a ship's main mast. It was known to dig its sharp, curved claws into boats, stare sailors in the face with its dinner plate–size eyeballs, and then drag them to the bottom of the sea without a second thought.

This is one seriously scary sea monster, but is it for real?

DENMARK
\—NORWAY
EUROPE

AFRICA

ARCTIC
OCEAN

NORWAY

Norwegian
Sea

SWEDEN

FINLAND

North
Sea

DENMARK

Colossal squid are armed with

TWO HUGE BEAKS AND ROTATING HOOKS

along their tentacles and can

G·R·O·W to be more than 40 feet (12.2 m) across!

THE DETAILS

THERE ARE REAL, live giant squid in our oceans. They were first described by a Danish naturalist in 1857 and have made rare (but memorable) appearances ever since. The biggest species of giant squid, called the colossal squid, is a squishy cephalopod. They live 6,560 feet (2,000 m) below the surface of Antarctic waters, so deep that scientists have never been able to study a live specimen. But could these grow to be the size of the kraken? From the bodies of colossal squid that wash up on shore, experts think they weigh about half a ton (453 kg) each. That's big, but not quite the size of the beast described by sailors.

HUMBOLDT SQUID,
ONE OF THE LARGEST
KNOWN SPECIES OF SQUID

THE CLUES

Could there be an even more monstrous creature lurking in the depths? See if you think there's a tentacle of truth to this legend.

▶ **SHIP SHUFFLE** In 1978, the crew aboard a U.S. Navy ship claimed their ship was damaged after a run-in with a mystery monster from the depths.

▶ **DISTURBANCE IN THE DEEP** In 2003, a group of fishermen in the icy Ross Sea (a deep, dark bay in Antarctica's Southern Ocean) encountered a cephalopod-like creature feeding on a Patagonian toothfish, which can grow up to 7.5 feet (2.3 m) in length. Was it really a colossal squid, or could it have been the kraken?

▶ **CLASH OF GIANTS** Whalers working in the Antarctic have reported seeing dramatic fights between colossal squid and giant sperm whales.

THE THEORIES

SOME BELIEVE the 1978 incident reported by the Navy ship could have been our pal, the kraken. Others believe there's no such thing as a kraken. There's no solid evidence that a super sea creature like kraken exists, or that it would eat anything other than fish if it does exist. One scientist says human fishers are actually doing more harm to the huge cephalopods that do exist, like the colossal squid, by depleting the ocean of fish that they need to eat. Boat-swallowing sea monsters, most experts agree, are not feeding on human sailors. But they do provide a fishy feast for our imaginations. Could a colossal squid be masquerading as that crazy kraken? Without more evidence and eyewitness accounts, we might never get to the depths of this mystery.

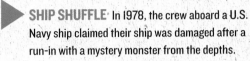
RINGED TENTACLES

WHAT HAS 50 FEET BUT CAN'T WALK?

THE BACKGROUND

1 **IN 1959,** a Belgian colonel flying a helicopter back from a mission deep in Africa's Congo had quite a fright when he noticed a giant, slithering supersnake on the ground below. But Colonel Van Lierde didn't let the snake rattle him. Instead, the pilot showed a lot of backbone, flying back and forth over the white-bellied behemoth so his passenger could snap some pics.

The spooky snake sighting started a mystery that's never been solved. What was that big, scary thing?

THE DETAILS

2 **THAT DAY,** Van Lierde—an experienced military pilot skilled in estimating the size of objects below while flying—saw what he believed was a 50-foot (15.2-m)-long, shiny dark green snake moving through the African bush. Watching from his helicopter 500 feet (152 m) above, he had a hard time believing his eyes. But the camera didn't lie. At one point, the snake reared up about

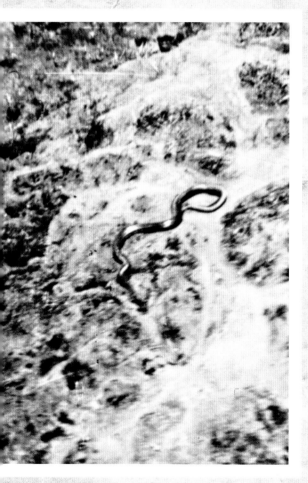

BELGIAN COLONEL REMY VAN LIERDE
snapped a shot of this supersize snake while flying over the Congo region in Africa in 1959. But just how big is this slithering specimen?

GREEN ANACONDA

10 feet (3 m), like it was trying to strike at the copter, but thankfully Van Lierde was flying too high for the creature to reach.

THE THEORIES

3 **NOT MANY SEEM TO DOUBT** the authenticity of this photograph or the snake in it. The tricky part is confirming the size of the creature. Are these blobs around the snake trees, bushes, or grasses? Without something to put it all in perspective, it's hard for experts to say for sure how big Van Lierde's snake actually was. Could the great snake have been a mismeasured rock python or a supersize green anaconda? Green anacondas are known to grow to more than 29 feet (8.8 m) long and 12 inches (30.5 cm) thick, and they can weigh more than 550 pounds (249 kg). One thing's for sure—this mystery has remained a tightly coiled secret.

NEW EVIDENCE REVEALED!

In 2007, a team of scientists discovered a fossil of a vertebrate from the Earth's largest snake ever in a coal mine in Colombia. It belonged to *Titanoboa cerrejonensis,* a massive extinct anaconda-like beast that slithered through steamy tropical rain forests about 60 million years ago. What's interesting is how much Van Lierde's snake resembles this snake, which scientists estimate was at least 42 feet (12.8 m) long—longer than a city bus—and weighed 2,500 pounds (1,134 kg).

4

FREAKY
PHENOMENA

WHAT IN THE WORLD? Have you ever seen something so bizarre that you had to stop and wonder, *Am I seeing things?* This chapter is chock-full of unexplainable stuff—from spectral spacemen selfies to screaming corpses, UFO sightings, and foreboding footprints. Scientists and sleuths are still scratching their heads over these mysteries. Read on for some hair-raising, spine-tingling cases from the past that'll make you say, "No way!"

THE SCREAMING MUMMY

WHY WAS
THIS GUY'S
FACE PRESERVED IN
PAIN?

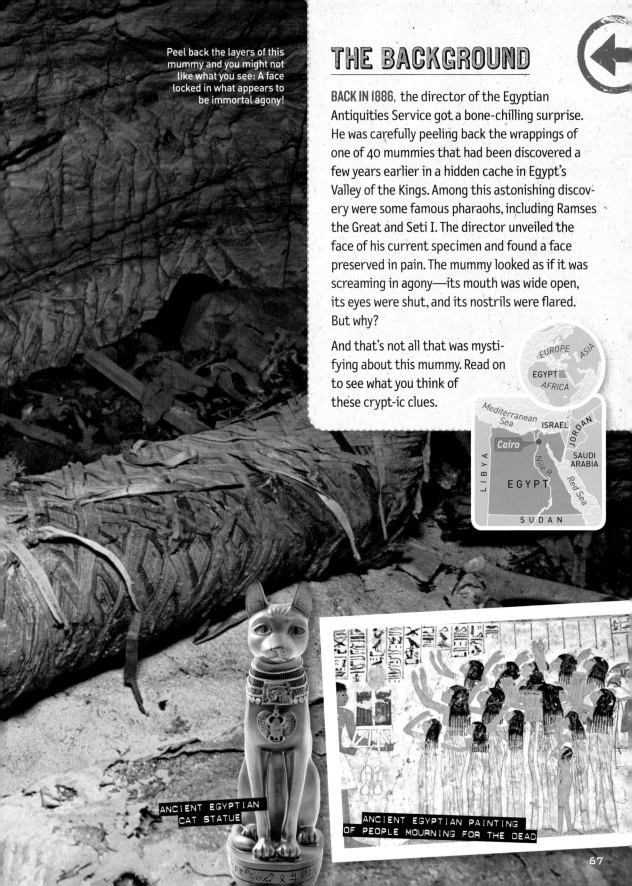

Peel back the layers of this mummy and you might not like what you see: A face locked in what appears to be immortal agony!

THE BACKGROUND

BACK IN 1886, the director of the Egyptian Antiquities Service got a bone-chilling surprise. He was carefully peeling back the wrappings of one of 40 mummies that had been discovered a few years earlier in a hidden cache in Egypt's Valley of the Kings. Among this astonishing discovery were some famous pharaohs, including Ramses the Great and Seti I. The director unveiled the face of his current specimen and found a face preserved in pain. The mummy looked as if it was screaming in agony—its mouth was wide open, its eyes were shut, and its nostrils were flared. But why?

And that's not all that was mystifying about this mummy. Read on to see what you think of these crypt-ic clues.

EUROPE ASIA
EGYPT AFRICA

Mediterranean Sea
ISRAEL
JORDAN
Cairo
LIBYA
EGYPT
SAUDI ARABIA
Nile R.
Red Sea
SUDAN

ANCIENT EGYPTIAN CAT STATUE

ANCIENT EGYPTIAN PAINTING OF PEOPLE MOURNING FOR THE DEAD

THE DETAILS

MUMMIFICATION is the process of preserving the skin and flesh of a corpse. Ancient Egyptians believed this process paves the way for a deceased person to travel to a peaceful afterlife. This screaming mummy's face wasn't the only puzzling thing about "unknown Man E." He was covered in sheepskin or goatskin, which is not a normal part of the mummification process, and he still had his internal organs within his body, which is also highly unusual. However, according to ancient Egyptian customs, mummification itself was usually reserved for nobility like royals or priests, so he was likely someone of great importance. So who was he? And why was he screaming?

ANCIENT EGYPTIAN LIMESTONE CARVING OF MOURNERS

THE CLUES

The questions surrounding this 3,000-year-old body, which is now at the Egyptian Museum in Cairo, Egypt, still baffle scientists. So far, "mum's" the word, but we do have a few clues about him:

▶ **ODD ORGANS** The body still contained internal organs including his brain and was not completely dehydrated like with a normal mummification. A physician who examined the mummy back in the late 1800s concluded that the mummy's stomach was contracted in a way that suggests he was poisoned.

▶ **MESSY MUMMY** Along with the sheepskin, a strange ancient and dried-out paste covered the body.

▶ **GRAVE TROUBLE** "Unknown Man E" was mummified with no grave marking or identification. Egyptians at the time would have believed the lack of identification at his burial site would have prevented him from moving on to a happy afterlife, which was unusual for the dead who were mummified.

THE THEORIES

GENERATIONS OF SCHOLARS have searched for answers about the mysterious identity of the screaming mummy and what happened to make him scream. Egyptologists agree he was not mummified in the usual way. The presence of the internal organs, the unusual paste covering him, and the fact that he wasn't completely dehydrated has led most experts to think he was a person of prominence who was being punished for doing something very bad. But what crime did he commit, and was he even Egyptian? In 2008, a team of scientists used sophisticated technology including CT scans, a facial reconstruction artist, and x-rays to try to shed light on the mystery. By combining the results from that technology and cross-referencing writings on ancient Egyptian papyrus scrolls, they believe the body could belong to Prince Pentewere, who, according to the scrolls, was suspected of working with his mother to plot the murder of his father, Pharaoh Ramses III. Since he was a member of the royal family, it's possible he was allowed to commit suicide, like by drinking poison, rather than face execution. Still, new evidence continues to emerge and some skeptics don't agree the body belongs to Pentewere. They think the body might not be Egyptian at all but instead could belong to a murdered rival foreign prince. Researchers are still unraveling clues on this one.

RAMSES III

Ancient Egyptians believed a **MUMMY** must be identified with the person's name for the person to reach the **AFTERLIFE.**

WHO LEFT THESE FRIGHTENING TRACKS IN THE GARDEN?

THE BACKGROUND

FOR 150 YEARS, people have wondered exactly who left a trail of devilish footprints in the snow in 1855 in Devon, England, U.K. In 2009, the freaky phenomenon happened all over again in the same area when a woman woke up one day to find a petrifying path of unidentifiable prints in the snow. The prints went through fences, over rooftops, and across rivers. Local legend says it was the devil walking. But was it?

No one has ever figured out who left the first trail of footprints. Now people are up at night wondering all over again. Make tracks to turn the page, if you dare, and see who—or what—you think left these spine-tingling tracks.

ATLANTIC
OCEAN
UNITED KINGDOM
North Sea
IRELAND
Devon
FRANCE

UNITED KINGDOM   EUROPE
AFRICA

What has hooves like a cow, walks upright like a human, and loves to walk in the snow every 150 years or so?

THE DETAILS

EVEN THOUGH THEY APPEARED mysteriously more than 150 years apart, both instances of these perplexing prints looked as if they were made from a cloven hoof, which means it had two "toes," like the hooves of a cow or a goat. Just one problem: Whoever left these marks appears to walk on two "feet"—not four. A zoologist measured the marks left in 2009 to be about five inches (12.7 cm) across.

THE CLUES

Modern science has helped experts get a foot in the door of solving this mystery. But the possibilities still give us the chills.

▶ **GHOSTLY PRINTS** The sets of footprints were strikingly similar. In 1855 and 2009, the footprints traveled about 100 miles (161 km) through the town of Devon, even appearing to go through haystacks, a 14-foot (4.3-m) wall, and locked gates; up drainpipes; across rooftops; and through the River Exe.

▶ **HOT TIP** Some witnesses reported that the prints had melted the snow as if they'd been made with something like hot iron, as opposed to having been made by an animal.

▶ **BIG STRIDES** So whoever or whatever left the tracks would have been very large. At the time, a newspaper reported that the animal would have had a stride between a foot (0.3 m) and one and a half feet (.46 m) long.

KANGAROOS belong to the animal family Macropus, which means "BIG FOOT."

Crunch, crunch, crunch. Who's walking there? A person? A horse? What if it's none of these things? These mysterious prints went over rooftops, across a river, and even up a drainpipe! But one question that has sidestepped experts so far: Who left these odd tracks in the snow, not once, but *twice*?

BADGER

DONKEYS

KANGAROOS

THE THEORIES

SCIENTISTS HAVE NEVER BEEN ABLE to confirm whether the mysterious tracks were made by a two- or four-legged creature. In 2009, the woman who found the tracks in her garden called the nearby Centre for Fortean Zoology (the word "fortean" refers to the paranormal). Because the tracks were so far apart, zoologists said the mysterious feet could belong to a rabbit. Others wondered if the tracks belonged to a donkey, a badger, a weather balloon dragging an anchor, or maybe even a mischievous kangaroo that had escaped from a private zoo! Unless this freaky phenomenon happens again, and the culprit is caught in the act, we may never know for sure who—or what—made these tracks.

THIS IS ONE
MOTHER SHIP
OF A
MYSTERY.

THE BACKGROUND

IN 1947, civilian pilot Kenneth Arnold reported a UFO (unidentified flying object) sighting while flying an airplane near Mount Rainier in Washington State, U.S.A. He said the nine shiny objects that he'd seen with his own eyes had the shape of teacup saucers, which is how the term "flying saucer" got its start. He estimated they were hovering about 25 miles (40.2 km) away from him. UFOs are often explained away as cases of mistaken identity or the imagination gone wild. But what Arnold witnessed, along with a UFO rumored to have landed the same year in Roswell, New Mexico, U.S.A., prompted the Air Force to launch an investigation and begin tracking UFO sightings.

Research on the subject might have taken off after Arnold's sensational sighting, but there were—and still are—many more questions than answers about his encounter.

WASHINGTON
UNITED STATES

CANADA
U.S.

PACIFIC OCEAN

WASHINGTON

IDAHO

Mt. Rainier

OREGON

THE DETAILS

KENNETH ARNOLD, MIDDLE

IN HIS ORIGINAL ACCOUNT of the event, Arnold described flying an airplane over the Cascade Mountains in Washington on June 24, 1947. The skies were clear and smooth as he headed toward Mount Rainier, which, at 14,411 feet (4,392 m), is the highest peak in the mountain range. That's when he noticed a reflection in the sky and then saw nine flying, glowing objects that emitted a blue-white light. His account of the unidentified flying objects inspired a whole new era of ufologists—people who search for, study, and talk about similar instances of UFOs and the extraterrestrial visitors they might carry.

THE CLUES

That day, Arnold provided lots of specific details about the objects he saw—which he estimated were 45 to 50 feet (13.7 to 15.2 m) across. They didn't spin or whirl, but instead flew fast in a fixed position, at about 1,700 miles an hour (2,736 km/h). What do you make of the clues below about these fantastic flying saucers?

▶ **FAST AND FURIOUS** Arnold could see the flying objects clearly against the backdrop of snow on the mountains. He estimated that they formed a "chain" about five miles (8 km) long.

▶ **NOT YOUR AVERAGE GEESE** Arnold reported that the objects flew in a V-formation, swerving in and out of the snow-covered mountains.

▶ **PERFECT SKIM-METRY** Arnold said the saucers bounced the same way a flat skipping rock skims the surface of water. He also noted that the aircraft were about 20 times wider than they were tall.

THE THEORIES

EVEN THOUGH ARNOLD originally reported that his story was "positively true" and he provided many specific details about what he saw, how the objects flew and approximately how fast, he later revised his story to say the "UFOs" were likely military aircraft. But the military said they had no record of test flights happening when the incident occurred. The Air Force investigated Arnold's report and declared that the whole episode had been a mirage, or an optical illusion created by weather conditions up in the air. On the other hand, during the 1940s, '50s, and '60s, the U.S. military set up a series of investigations, the most famous of which was Project Blue Book. It concluded that 94 percent of the 12,000 or so UFO sightings it investigated could be identified as things like aircraft, weather balloons, birds, meteors, or other planets (some were found to be photos of pie plates!). But that still leaves 6 percent, including Arnold's UFOs, still undeniably unidentifiable!

Among the people who have claimed to see a **UFO** is former U.S. president **JIMMY CARTER.**

When pilot Kenneth Arnold first saw the spheres sailing through the sky, he thought he was seeing a reflection of something that sunny day.

ANCIENT
COMPUTER
BAFFLES
SCIENTISTS.

SPONGE DIVERS
MAKE A DAMP
DISCOVERY.

The Antikythera mechanism predicted **ECLIPSES** using an 18-year eclipse cycle, called the **SAROS CYCLE.**

REPLICA ANTIKYTHERA MECHANISM

THE BACKGROUND

IN 1901, sponge divers in the ocean near the Greek island of Antikythera discovered a rustic relic that researchers later determined to be the world's first computer. You're probably thinking "that's impossible!" Well, technically, a computer can be defined as a device that stores and processes data. In 2016, one historian told the *Washington Post* newspaper that this find was the "single most information-rich object that has been uncovered by archaeologists from ancient times."

Of course, the ancient device didn't work after spending centuries getting soggy at the bottom of the sea. The original is so corroded that a replica was made to better see the details of the device. But who built this amazingly advanced contraption, and what was it built to do?

ATLANTIC OCEAN
EUROPE
GREECE
AFRICA

MACEDONIA
ALBANIA
Ionian Sea
GREECE
Aegean Sea
TURKEY
Phaistos Palace, Crete
Sea of Crete
Mediterranean Sea

This
MIGHTY
MECHANISM
is more complex than some clocks developed
MORE THAN 1,000 YEARS later.

THE DETAILS

RESEARCHERS DATED the waterlogged device as from around 150 to 100 B.C. But who made it, and what was it used for?

THE CLUES

Scientists are still tinkering with this ancient computer to uncover its mysteries. Here's how it might have worked:

▶ **GEARING UP** When scientists examined this amazing find, they discovered it was powered by a hand crank, with layers of bronze gears with interlocking ridges and dials.

▶ **SUNKEN TREASURES** The underwater artifact was mixed up with other treasures—bronze sculptures, jewels, and coins—from an ancient Roman merchant ship that sank.

▶ **WASHED-UP WORDS** X-ray technology has recently revealed text from within the mechanism that contains more than 3,400 Greek characters.

COLOSSVS SOLIS.

ARTIST'S DEPICTION OF A MASSIVE ANCIENT STATUE ON RHODES

STARRY SKY

THE THEORIES

BECAUSE IT WAS FOUND along with other artifacts from a sunken Roman merchant ship, experts think that when the Antikythera mechanism was plunged into the ocean, it was on its way to be sold at a Roman port. An international team of archaeologists, astronomers, and historians have studied the mechanism and determined that the complex, clock like instrument likely told time and the movement of planets and stars. Some think this device could have helped sports fans track the cyclical schedule of ancient athletic contests—including the Olympic Games! Scientists speculate that they have about one-fifth of the text that was originally part of this ancient device. When translated, the text has included mentions of a calendar, references to Spain, and even a sporting event held in the ancient city of Rhodes on a Greek island. Despite all the things that we don't know about this clever contraption, one thing we do know is that the Greeks were onto something super-scientific and sophisticated for their time.

INSCRIPTIONS ON THE ANTIKYTHERA MECHANISM

THIS MYSTERY HAS GOTTEN OUT OF HAND.

THE BACKGROUND

IN THE WESTERN DESERT OF EGYPT, a prehistoric rocky shelter hides an intriguing surprise. Hundreds of mysterious, unusually tiny humanlike handprints. It also includes ancient paintings of animals, people, and odd headless beings. Here comes the spine-tingling part: The handprints include oddly long fingers, too long to be human. Researchers—who might have been the first people in thousands of years to view these ancient paintings—discovered the place in 2002. It was later named Wadi Sura II, and it is also known as the "cave of beasts."

Whose prints are on these cave walls and why? Are these handprints human, or ... something else?

These ancient handprints discovered in a cave in Africa might look pretty human to you upon first glance, but don't be fooled. Experts say the ratio of finger length to hand length is decidedly not human. So who—or what—left them behind?

THE DETAILS

RESEARCHERS BELIEVE the "handprints" are between 6,000 and 8,000 years old. A team of anthropologists compared measurements of the ancient handprints, which measure approximately 1.5 inches (3.8 cm) to 2 inches (5.1 cm) long, with the dimensions of human infants' hands. They came up with more questions than answers.

THE CLUES

Until this discovery, ancient stenciled hands and feet of very small children had been seen in Australian rock art, but never in the Sahara. And if the prints don't match the dimensions of human infants, then what on Earth—or beyond—made them?

▶ **FLEXIBLE DESIGN** The tiny handprints on the wall vary, indicating that whatever made them was flexible, not fixed like wood or clay.

▶ **REPTILE HANDS** Researchers noted that the species with the most similar "hands" to the prints on the wall are desert monitor lizards and baby crocodiles.

▶ **GETTING CREATIVE** On the ancient rock wall, even smaller baby-like hands appear inside some of the tiny handprints.

One sweet scene in **WADI SURA II** shows one pair of **BABY "HANDS"** nestled inside another pair.

A desert can keep a secret for thousands of years—like who left their handprints all over these ancient walls. Other cave art discovered in the same region shows more detailed images, such as giraffes and even people.

THE THEORIES

ANTHROPOLOGIST EMMANUELLE HONORÉ of the McDonald Institute for Archaeological Research studied and measured the hands of real babies. Based on her research, she does not believe the handprints in the cave are human. She suspected the little hand-prints might be monkey paws but later deduced they most resembled reptile feet. Some experts believe the prehistoric people who created this art severed the feet of these animals to "stamp" the imprints on the walls. They believe the prints may have been created as ancient human art-ists blew pigment made from animal or plant matter around these stamps. Others believe they are naturally occurring footprints from animals. Some think they could be from other-worldly beings. If only walls could talk, then maybe we'd have an answer.

IS THIS SUSPICIOUS SPACEMAN FOR REAL?

THE BACKGROUND

1 **TALK ABOUT A PHOTOBOMB!** When a dad named Jim Templeton took a picture of his little girl holding flowers in an empty field in 1964, he got more than he asked for. After developing the film, the photograph showed his daughter smiling, sitting in the field, as expected. What wasn't expected was that the photo also showed a strange being in what appeared to be a space suit standing in the field right behind her!

For nearly 50 years, debate has swirled around this far-out photo and who's in it. Did a person from space drop in for a visit?

THE DETAILS

2 **TEMPLETON CLAIMS** that on the sunny, clear day he snapped the pic, no one else was in the area. The field they were in overlooks the Solway Firth (a channel in the sea) at the border between England and Scotland. The incident made international headlines in the 1960s, during the time of the famous space exploration race between the Soviet Union and the United States. In fact, Russian cosmonaut Yuri Gagarin had just become the first person in space in 1961, just a few years earlier.

THE THEORIES

3 **UFOLOGISTS** (people who study UFOs) took the photo as a clear sign that there were aliens in space suits among us. Even Jim Templeton may have believed something otherworldly was in that picture of his daughter. Others claimed it was a ghost. Some suggest it was a fairy.

THE PEACEFUL and picturesque Solway Firth in Scotland, U.K., where Templeton took his far-out photo

THE PEACEFUL and picturesque Solway Firth in Scotland, U.K., where Templeton took his far-out photo

NEW EVIDENCE REVEALED!

Modern photo analysis has now led experts to believe that the mysterious being in the picture is actually Templeton's wife, who wandered into the frame without Templeton realizing it. They think his camera's flash made the back of her dress appear like a white space suit and her hair look like part of an astronaut's helmet. It looks like this mystery just came crashing down to Earth.

MYSTIFYING MONUMENTS

THESE STELLAR SUPERSTRUCTURES have stood the test of time. We've got rock formations, one big stone cat, carved messages, and mega-men half buried in the dirt. But what do they mean? What were they used for? Who made them and how? One thing's for sure, someone went to a lot of trouble to construct them, which tells us they were very important to whoever built them. By examining these towering tributes, we can learn about ancient civilizations and decode some puzzles of the past. But some statues sometimes just leave us scratching our heads.

People have wondered about Stonehenge, one of the world's most intriguing mysteries, for thousands of years. Some say it may have taken prehistoric workers about 30 million hours to build it.

THE CASE:
EASTER ISLAND

WHO CARVED THESE HEADS AND WHY?

▸ THE BACKGROUND

ON A REMOTE ISLAND off the coast of Chile called Easter Island (the Earth's most isolated spot inhabited by humans), an army of ancient monoliths has been guarding the island for centuries. The word "monolith" refers to a massive single stone, often standing upright as a monument. Ancient islanders—likely transplants from Polynesia between A.D. 300 and 400—carved more than 1,000 of the massive figures, which were then situated to ring the island, facing inland. Called moai (sounds like MOE-eye), each one stands on a sacred platform called an *ahu* (sounds like AH-hoo).

A heady mystery has been in the air for centuries about who carved these guys, how they got to the island, and what is the purpose of the statues. Can we wrap our head around this mystery?

NORTH AMERICA

ATLANTIC OCEAN

PACIFIC OCEAN

SOUTH AMERICA

CHILE

Easter Island

ANTARCTICA

Some of the MOAI have torsos that you can't see because the figures are BURIED UP TO their necks.

THE DETAILS

THE STATUES WERE DISCOVERED about 300 years ago by European explorers. Island lore says the statues are infused with the spirits of the inhabitants' ancestors. While the buildup of sediment over time has buried some of the moai, today there are still some 900 of these giant statues watching and protecting the island (others have been destroyed by erosion and weather). One thing they're not doing—speaking up about how they were built, their symbolic meaning, or how anybody moved these monstrous monoliths into place without modern machinery and equipment.

THE CLUES

The mega moai weigh about 26,000 pounds (11,800 kg) each. How ancient people—with no access to metal tools or even wheels (which hadn't been invented yet)—made them and moved them into place is a mystery. These clues only seem to create more questions than answers:

▶ **MEGA-MEN** The many moai men were carved (using only hand tools) from porous, lightweight volcanic rock. But at an average of 13 feet (4 m) high, they are certainly not lightweight!

▶ **ON YOUR OWN TWO FEET** Oral tradition says the statues walked themselves into place.

▶ **TEXT MESSAGE** Along with the many moai, researchers found wooden and stone tablets filled with mysterious script, called rongorongo.

In the local language, **EASTER ISLAND** is called **RAPA NUI.**

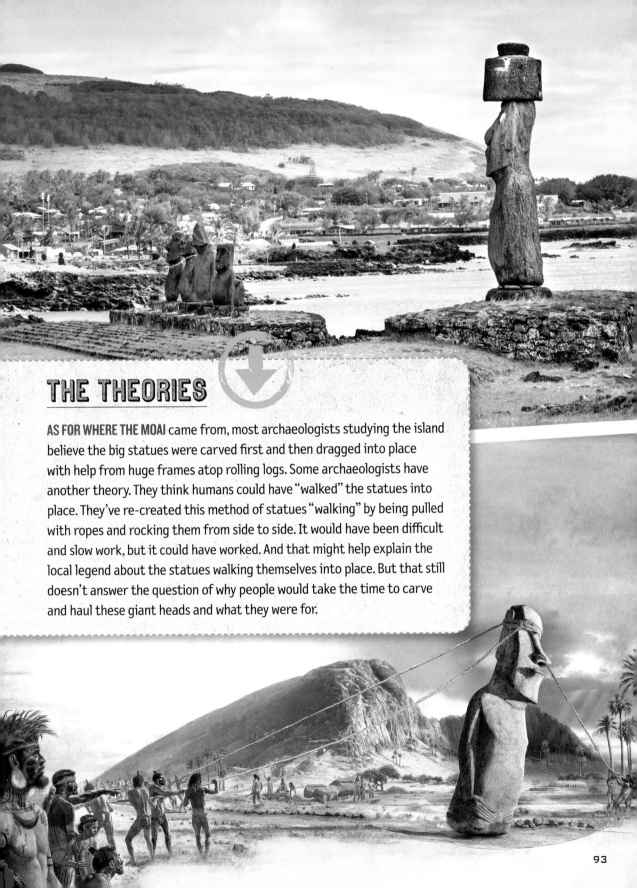

THE THEORIES

AS FOR WHERE THE MOAI came from, most archaeologists studying the island believe the big statues were carved first and then dragged into place with help from huge frames atop rolling logs. Some archaeologists have another theory. They think humans could have "walked" the statues into place. They've re-created this method of statues "walking" by being pulled with ropes and rocking them from side to side. It would have been difficult and slow work, but it could have worked. And that might help explain the local legend about the statues walking themselves into place. But that still doesn't answer the question of why people would take the time to carve and haul these giant heads and what they were for.

THE CASE:
SPHINX OF GIZA

THIS
COOL CAT
HAS STUMPED
SCIENTISTS FOR
CENTURIES.

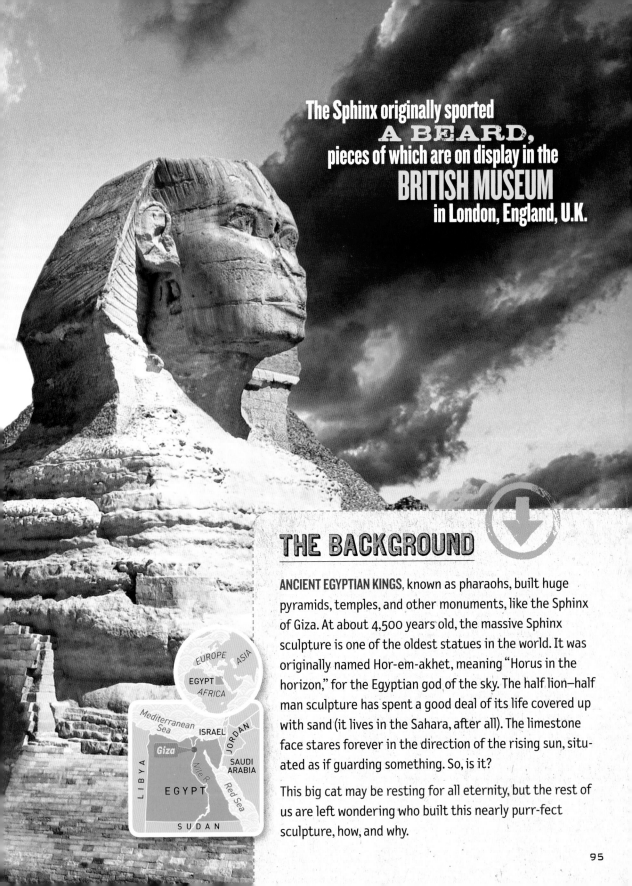

The Sphinx originally sported **A BEARD**, pieces of which are on display in the **BRITISH MUSEUM** in London, England, U.K.

THE BACKGROUND

ANCIENT EGYPTIAN KINGS, known as pharaohs, built huge pyramids, temples, and other monuments, like the Sphinx of Giza. At about 4,500 years old, the massive Sphinx sculpture is one of the oldest statues in the world. It was originally named Hor-em-akhet, meaning "Horus in the horizon," for the Egyptian god of the sky. The half lion–half man sculpture has spent a good deal of its life covered up with sand (it lives in the Sahara, after all). The limestone face stares forever in the direction of the rising sun, situated as if guarding something. So, is it?

This big cat may be resting for all eternity, but the rest of us are left wondering who built this nearly purr-fect sculpture, how, and why.

THE DETAILS

THE FIRST PEOPLE to live on the banks of Egypt's Nile River were hunters and fishermen who settled in the area more than 8,000 years ago. By 3000 B.C., a sophisticated civilization had been established, led by rich and powerful pharaohs. They built monuments like the Pyramids at Giza, which are considered one of the wonders of the world. At 66 feet (20 m) tall, the Sphinx is almost as tall as the White House in Washington, D.C. It has paws bigger than a city bus and was carved from a single enormous piece of limestone. You can help solve the riddle of the Sphinx.

THE CLUES

To create this supercool desert cat, you'd need a lot of help and access to a lot of resources. So who had access to lots of laborers and materials? Pharaohs, for sure. But why did they spend what must have been generations building this enormous awe-inspiring structure in the desert?

▶ **A SURPRISING DISCOVERY** In 1990, a tourist stumbled on part of an ancient cemetery. Researchers discovered hundreds of bodies, many identified as laborers thanks to still legible inscriptions.

▶ **ALL DRESSED UP** The Sphinx wears the headdress of the great Egyptian pharaohs.

▶ **A BIG STATEMENT** In Arabic, the Sphinx of Giza is called the "father of terror." Many Egyptologists date the statue back to about 2500 B.C., which was around the reign of Pharaoh Khafre. Khafre was known for building the second pyramid of Giza and, in at least one ancient account, was said to be a cruel ruler.

Ancient Egyptians lived and worked on the banks of the Nile River in Egypt, not far from the Pyramids at Giza.

THE THEORIES

EGYPTOLOGISTS, geologists, and archaeologists have spent years trying to understand the mysteries of the Sphinx. Most scholars believe it was built by Pharaoh Khafre, or possibly for him. He ruled Egypt around 2600 B.C. If he was indeed a tyrannical ruler, the name "father of terror" for the statue certainly makes sense. He would have had access to thousands of laborers to do the backbreaking work of building the huge statue, which may be a tribute to a lion god that guarded the horizon. Some even speculate that the statue was built to guard the final resting place of some ancient yet still undiscovered pharaoh buried somewhere close by!

ALIENS
ACTIVITY
AREA

THE SPHINX

DOES THIS SURPRISE
STRUCTURE HOLD
MONUMENTAL
MESSAGES
FOR THE
WORLD?

THE BACKGROUND

IN 1980, ON A HILL IN ELBERTON, GEORGIA, U.S.A., about two hours from Atlanta, a 19-foot (5.8-m)-tall sculpture suddenly appeared. It had a very long message engraved on the surface, translated in many different languages—including some ancient ones! The message lists 10 principles, such as "Maintain humanity under 500,000,000 in perpetual balance with nature" and "Prize truth—beauty—love—seeking harmony with the infinite."

Theories surrounding this large peace-promoting masterpiece abound. Where did it come from? Who put it there and why?

UNITED STATES
GEORGIA

TENN.

Elberton

SOUTH CAROLINA

ALABAMA

GEORGIA

ATLANTIC OCEAN

FLORIDA

DUMISHA BI
(MIA) TANC
KULINGAN

ONGOZA UZA
ENEZA AF

TUNGA LUGH
BINAADAM
TULIZA HAM
MAMBO YC
LINDA WATU
KWA SHER

MATAIFA YO
NA VATATU
KWENYE KC

ACHILIA MAT
LINGANISHA
MATAIFA

TUNZA UKWE
TAFUTA US

KUSIWE NA N
IPE MAUME
IPE MAU

The mysterious GEORGIA GUIDESTONES are said to weigh more than 237,000 pounds (107,500 kg), which is about the weight of an adult BLUE WHALE.

Some people refer to the mysterious, massive Georgia Guidestones as the American Stonehenge.

THE DETAILS

THE SCULPTURE is made up of five granite slabs. But who put them there in 1980 without being seen, and why didn't they sign their work after going to all that trouble?

THE CLUES

There's not much to guide people on the meaning of these granite "guidestones," but these clues give a bit of an inside scoop:

▶ **WISE WORDS** Translated, the message at the top of the Georgia Guidestones means, "Let these be guidestones to an age of reason."

▶ **REAL OR FAKE?** A mystery man supposedly used a pseudonym (a fake name), R. C. Christian, to commission the expensive statue. He was reported to be an "elegantly dressed, gray-haired, middle-aged man." The granite company hired to build the guidestones originally thought the request was a prank.

▶ **ENIGMATIC ENGRAVINGS** The "capstone," or the slab that lies on top of this monument, has a single message engraved in four ancient languages—Babylon cuneiform, classical Greek, Sanskrit, and Egyptian hieroglyphs. The messages on the front of the stones (one says "Be not a cancer on the Earth, leave room for nature") are each engraved in eight modern languages, including Chinese, Hindi, and Russian.

ПУСТЬ ЗЕМНОЕ НАСЕЛЕНИЕ НИКОГДА
НЕ ПРЕВЫШАЕТ 500 000 000
ПРЕБЫВАЯ В ПОСТОЯННОМ
РАВНОВЕСИИ С ПРИРОДОЙ

РАЗУМНО РЕГУЛИРУЙТЕ РОЖДАЕМОСТЬ
ПОВЫШАЯ ЦЕННОСТЬ ЖИЗНЕННОЙ
ПОДГОТОВКИ И МНОГООБРАЗИЯ
ЧЕЛОВЕЧЕСТВА

НАЙДЕМ НОВЫЙ ЖИВОЙ ЯЗЫК
СПОСОБНЫЙ ОБЪЕДИНИТЬ
ЧЕЛОВЕЧЕСТВО

ПРОЯВЛЯЙТЕ ТЕРПИМОСТЬ
В ВОПРОСАХ ЧУВСТВ ВЕРЫ
ТРАДИЦИЙ И ИМ ПОДОБНЫХ

ПУСТЬ СПРАВЕДЛИВЫЕ ЗАКОНЫ
И БЕСПРИСТРАСТНЫЙ СУД ВСТАНУТ
НА ЗАЩИТУ НАРОДОВ И НАЦИЙ

ПУСТЬ КАЖДАЯ НАЦИЯ
САМА РЕШАЕТ СВОИ ВНУТРЕННИЕ
ДЕЛА, ВЫНОСЯ НА МИРОВОЙ СУД
ОБЩЕНАРОДНЫЕ ПРОБЛЕМЫ.

ИЗБЕГАЙТЕ МЕЛОЧНЫХ СУДЕБНЫХ ТЯЖБ
И БЕСПОЛЕЗНЫХ ЧИНОВНИКОВ.

ПОДДЕРЖИВАЙТЕ РАВНОВЕСИЕ
МЕЖДУ ЛИЧНЫМИ ПРАВАМИ
И ОБЩЕСТВЕННЫМИ ОБЯЗАНОСТЯМИ.

ПРЕВЫШЕ ВСЕГО ЦЕНИТЕ ПРАВДУ
КРАСОТУ ЛЮБОВЬ СТРЕМЯСЬ К
ГАРМОНИИ С БЕСКОНЕЧНОСТЬЮ

НЕ БУДЬТЕ РАКОМ ДЛЯ ЗЕМЛИ
ПРИРОДЕ ТОЖЕ
ОСТАВЬТЕ МЕСТО

THE THEORIES

JUST ABOUT EVERYBODY in Elberton has an idea about the meaning of the Georgia Guidestones. Some say the monument is a primer for life after a nuclear war. Others say it's a warning about the increasing population of people on the planet. Some even speculate that it was put in place by a time traveler from the future trying to save humanity! Still, to others, it's a spot to renew one's faith in their religion. Local businesses are on board, too. They want to create a festival around the guidestones to increase tourism in the area. Still, the mystery builder remains ... well, a mystery.

CIRCULAR STRUCTURE UNDER THE SEA

THIS MYSTERY STARTED OUT AS A BLIP ON THE RADAR.

The beautiful Sea of Galilee is in northeastern Israel, not far from the country's borders with Syria and Jordan.

THE BACKGROUND

WHAT'S TWICE THE SIZE of Stonehenge and stuck 30 feet (9.1 m) under the Sea of Galilee in Israel? It's a mysterious circular structure that's thousands of years old. Geophysicists, people who study the Earth, discovered the amazing ancient structure by accident in 2003. They were using sonar to research ancient pebbles on the bottom of the lake when what they thought was a massive pile of stones caught their attention.

So what is this sunken structure and how did it get to the bottom of an ancient lake? The answers to these questions seem to have been buried in the sea along with the structure itself.

EUROPE ASIA
ISRAEL—
AFRICA

Sea of Galilee   SYRIA
Mediterranean
Sea   ISRAEL   Dead Sea
JORDAN
EGYPT

The **SEA OF GALILEE** is actually a huge freshwater lake, and at **64 square miles** (166 sq km), it's almost **THREE TIMES THE SIZE** of Manhattan!

THE DETAILS

WHEN IT WAS DISCOVERED, researchers thought the supersize structure was just a large pile of stones. But after scuba diving down to check it out, they were able to conclude, based on the structure's shape, composition, and the fact that it doesn't look like any known natural feature, that it was man-made. Scientists refer to a structure like this as a "cairn," or a memorial created with a mound of stones. But what is it memorializing? At about three stories tall and weighing as much as 120,000 pounds (54,000 kg)—which is the same as a modern mega cruise ship—the structure is about twice the size of Stonehenge. It was built with large volcanic basalt stones, some weighing as much as 200 pounds (90.7 kg) each!

THE CLUES

Why would someone bother making a huge underwater monument? Or is the structure part of some long-lost city that was submerged? Underwater researchers have put their swimming skills to the test to bring up these important clues:

▶ **NEIGHBORING CITIES** Israeli researchers believe that the structure dates back more than 4,000 years and was built around the same time as other structures, monuments, and settlements found nearby on land.

▶ **SEA-RIOUS SMARTS** Whoever built this mysterious mound under the sea would have had some serious labor and organization skills.

▶ **VAGUE AGE** Some archaeologists estimate the structure to be anywhere between 2,000 and 12,000 years old.

THE THEORIES

FIGURING OUT THE AGE of a pile of stones under the sea is no easy feat and researchers are still looking for evidence that will help narrow down the age of the structure, such as man-made artifacts discovered at the site. One ancient city known to use stone circles in their architecture was located some 19 miles (30.6 km) away, but it is more than 4,000 years old. Could those people have created this mysterious stone structure? Other researchers are looking to another city, called Bet Yerah, located just a mile (1.6 km) to the south. Bet Yerah flourished about 4,000 years ago and was one of the most powerful cities in its region at that time. Leaders there would have had access to the sophisticated organizational skills, labor, and funds needed to create such a structure like this one. One thing experts agree on is that it must have been a very important site because it was so costly and labor-intensive to create. But what was it for? Without more concrete evidence to link the origins of this mysterious structure to a more specific time frame, it's hard to know which ancient civilization created it, or for what purpose. Researchers plan to do more excavation to uncover some answers.

BASALT BOULDERS UNDERWATER

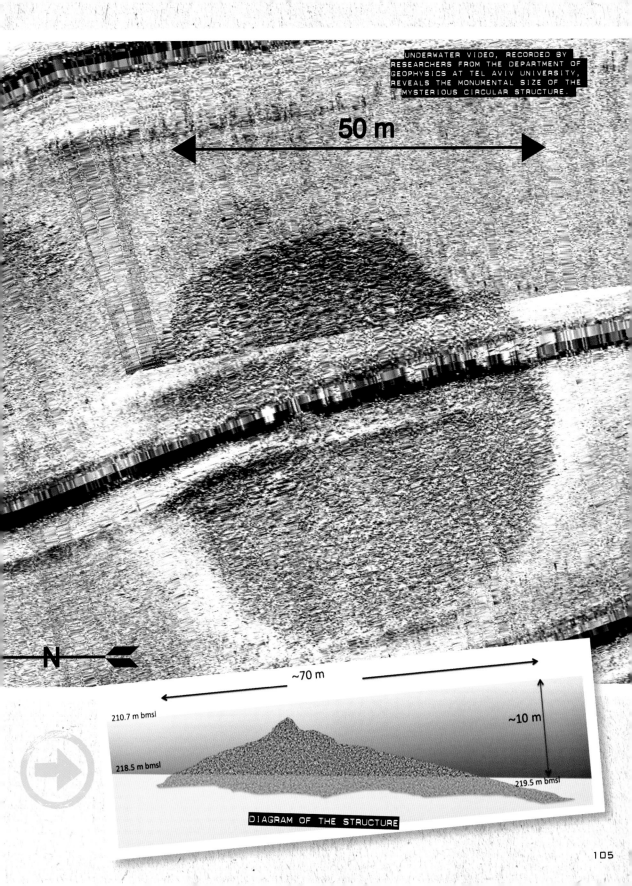

UNDERWATER VIDEO, RECORDED BY RESEARCHERS FROM THE DEPARTMENT OF GEOPHYSICS AT TEL AVIV UNIVERSITY, REVEALS THE MONUMENTAL SIZE OF THE MYSTERIOUS CIRCULAR STRUCTURE.

50 m

N

~70 m

210.7 m bmsl

~10 m

218.5 m bmsl

219.5 m bmsl

DIAGRAM OF THE STRUCTURE

WHAT'S THE PURPOSE OF THESE ROCKS?

STONEHENGE was made from rocks like these, found in a rocky outcrop of granite in England's Pembrokeshire region.

THE BACKGROUND

① **STONEHENGE IS PROBABLY** the most famous relic of prehistory in Europe, and it's one of the most studied set of ruins in the world. This ghostly circle of massive stones—some broken, some still standing—has towered above southern England's windswept Salisbury Plain for 4,500 years.

But the thing about Stonehenge is all the questions. Like why are the stones standing there? And how were the immensely heavy stones even carried into place? The closest place to find that kind of volcanic rock is almost 200 miles (322 km) away! So how did builders get those huge slabs all the way to where Stonehenge stands today?

THE DETAILS

② **FROM AFAR**, these giant towers of stone look more like a jumble of big rocks than an impressive monument. But up close, the staggering size of the stones mesmerizes. The largest of the stones

looms more than 30 feet (9.1 m) high and weighs more than 88,000 pounds (40,000 kg). They stand together in a circular pattern, almost making the stones look like sentries, or guardians.

THE THEORIES

3 **THEORIES ABOUND** about this strange circle of stones. Some say it was built as a center of human sacrifice. Some experts say it was built as a place of sun worship. Others say it was a temple for healing. One of the most popular theories is that Stonehenge was some sort of giant astronomical calendar, particularly because it was built on a place now called Salisbury Plain, a 300-square-mile (775-sq-km) grassy plateau that's long been said to be a sacred site. These theories explain what Stonehenge was used for, but not how the stones got there!

NEW EVIDENCE REVEALED!

In 2015, scientists announced that they had uncovered a sunken road that they believe was a route from an ancient stone quarry, which is where they think the Stonehenge stones are from. Workers from prehistoric times would have had to haul the massive volcanic rocks about 180 miles (290 km) from what is today the Preseli Hills in north Pembrokeshire, Wales, U.K., to where the monument stands today. Modern experts think they probably used stone hammers, wooden rollers, and levers to shape, transport, and erect Stonehenge's pieces.

CRYPTIC CODES & LOST LANGUAGES

How this creative clock in Berlin works could provide insight into solving codes like the baffling brainteaser called "Kryptos."

BEING A CODE BREAKER sounds pretty cool, eh? Well, the technical name for a professional code breaker is a cryptographer. Cryptographers spend hours, days, years, or even their whole lifetimes trying to decode mysterious texts and languages. They work with mathematicians, linguists, and historians to pick apart clues and uncover hidden messages. Think you have what it takes to be a breaker of codes? How about if the code was written thousands of years ago? Let's see just how hard it can be!

WHAT DOES THIS PIECE OF CLAY SAY?

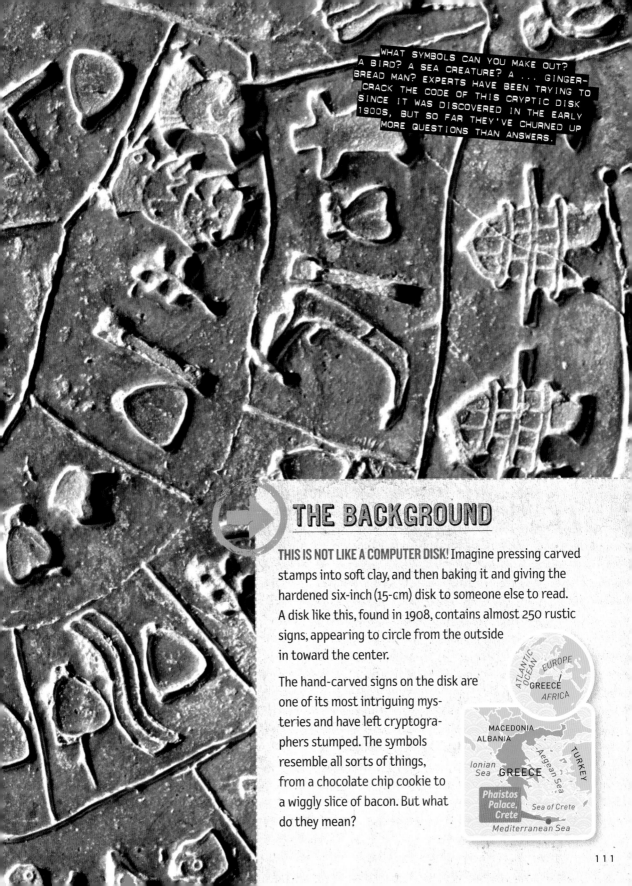

WHAT SYMBOLS CAN YOU MAKE OUT? A BIRD? A SEA CREATURE? A ... GINGER-BREAD MAN? EXPERTS HAVE BEEN TRYING TO CRACK THE CODE OF THIS CRYPTIC DISK SINCE IT WAS DISCOVERED IN THE EARLY 1900S, BUT SO FAR THEY'VE CHURNED UP MORE QUESTIONS THAN ANSWERS.

THE BACKGROUND

THIS IS NOT LIKE A COMPUTER DISK! Imagine pressing carved stamps into soft clay, and then baking it and giving the hardened six-inch (15-cm) disk to someone else to read. A disk like this, found in 1908, contains almost 250 rustic signs, appearing to circle from the outside in toward the center.

The hand-carved signs on the disk are one of its most intriguing mysteries and have left cryptographers stumped. The symbols resemble all sorts of things, from a chocolate chip cookie to a wiggly slice of bacon. But what do they mean?

ATLANTIC OCEAN
EUROPE
GREECE
AFRICA

MACEDONIA
ALBANIA
Ionian Sea
GREECE
Aegean Sea
TURKEY
Phaistos Palace, Crete
Sea of Crete
Mediterranean Sea

MINOAN ART

THE DETAILS

THE DISK WAS DISCOVERED by an Italian archaeologist in the ruins of an ancient palace on the hilly earthquake-prone Greek island of Crete. The disk is estimated to be roughly 4,000 years old, created at the end of the Stone Age by the Minoans, who lived on the island at that time. Known for "writing" on clay tablets, they were skilled in agriculture and making pottery.

THE CLUES

Few clay tablets like this have survived over the ages. Researchers think the text on the disk is made up of patterns of symbols that represent words. But what do they say? What do you make of this conundrum of communication?

▶ **SIGN LANGUAGE** The disk contains 45 unique symbols. One looks like a man with a Mohawk. Others resemble a hammer, a cat, a flower, a bird, a fish, and a fire hydrant.

▶ **WOMEN'S WORDS** In 2007, one expert researcher claimed to have decoded some of the symbols and thinks they say things like "mother" and "great lady of importance."

▶ **SERIOUS SYMBOLS** Some symbols appear to have been erased and restamped while the disks of clay were still soft.

THE THEORIES

FOR MORE THAN 100 YEARS, scientists have been digging, decoding, deciphering, and debating exactly what this ancient script means. One researcher, Dr. Gareth Owens, calls the Phaistos Disk a "Minoan CD-ROM," but he doubts that anyone has really fully understood the scope of the mysterious message. He does believe, however, that it's a tribute to someone's mother. Some say the writing (the script is referred to as Linear A) reflects a prayer to the mother goddess of the Minoan, but nobody really knows for sure. We may never know whether the message that the curious, Stone Age disk holds is about birds, bacon, or something much more serious.

PHAISTOS DISK

NO OTHER ARTIFACT
in the world has ever been found with the
WITH THE SAME SYMBOLS
AS THE PHAISTOS DISK.

The Phaistos disk was discovered in this hillside region of the Greek island Crete.

THE CASE: VOYNICH MANUSCRIPT

WHAT SECRETS DOES THIS BOOK HOLD?

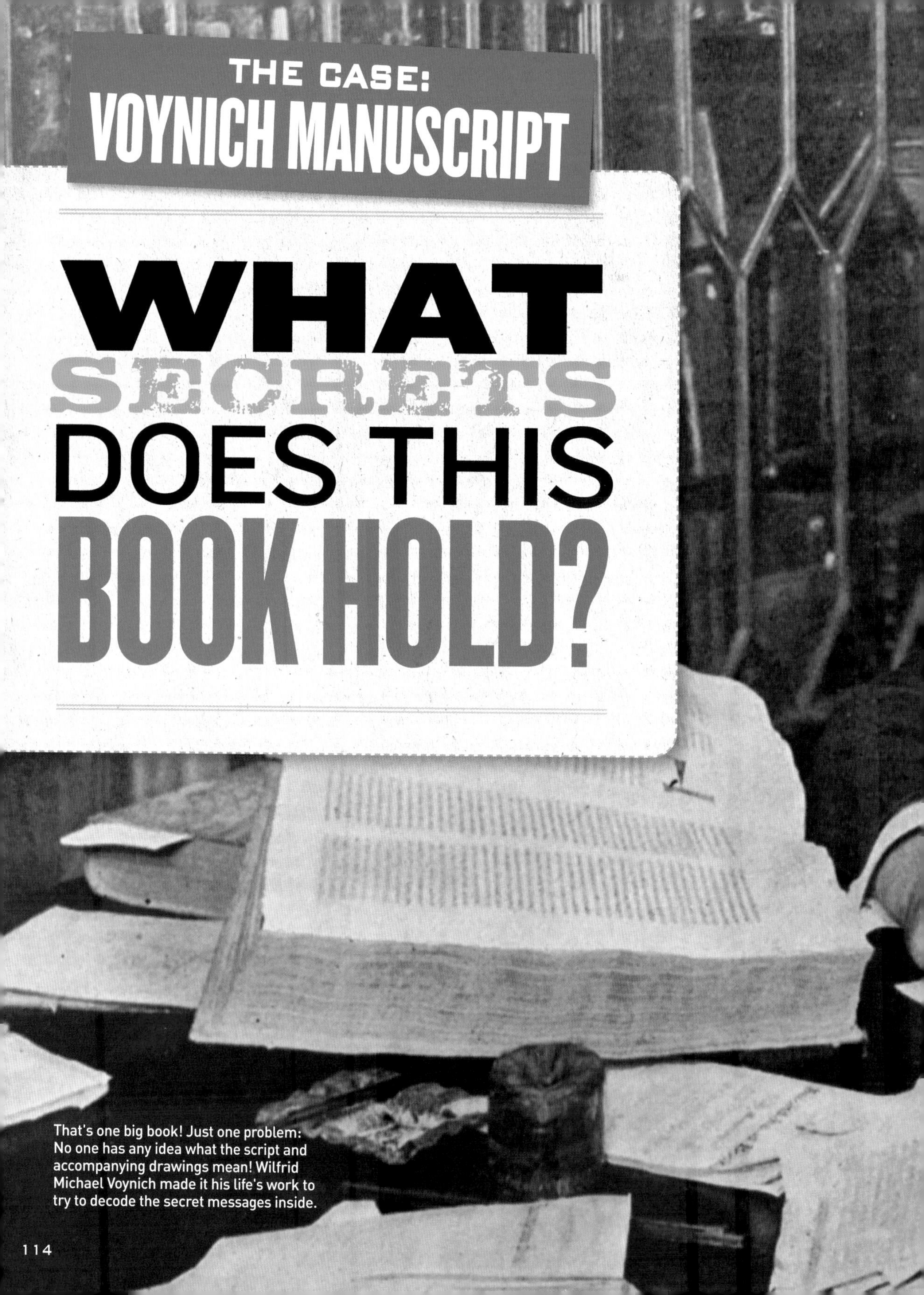

That's one big book! Just one problem: No one has any idea what the script and accompanying drawings mean! Wilfrid Michael Voynich made it his life's work to try to decode the secret messages inside.

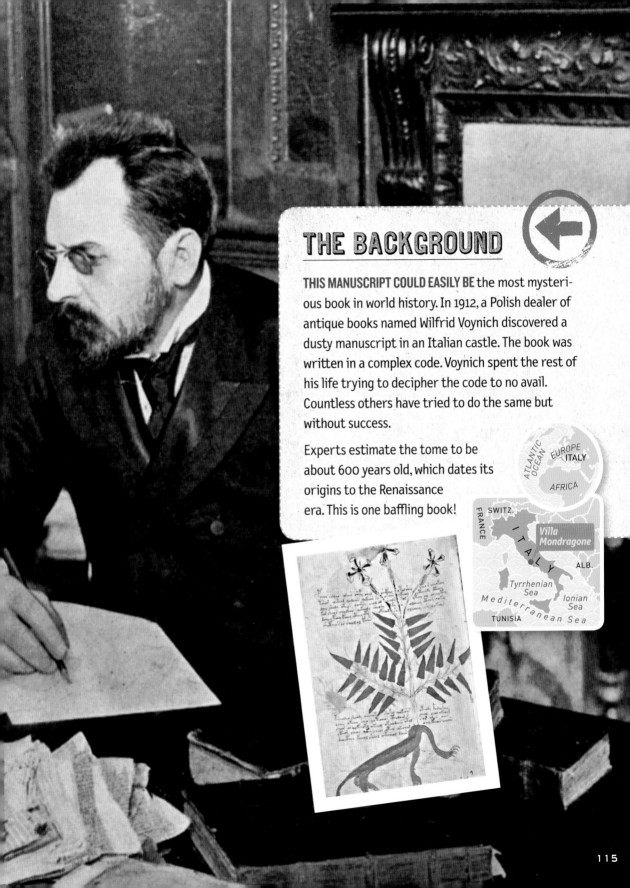

THE BACKGROUND

THIS MANUSCRIPT COULD EASILY BE the most mysterious book in world history. In 1912, a Polish dealer of antique books named Wilfrid Voynich discovered a dusty manuscript in an Italian castle. The book was written in a complex code. Voynich spent the rest of his life trying to decipher the code to no avail. Countless others have tried to do the same but without success.

Experts estimate the tome to be about 600 years old, which dates its origins to the Renaissance era. This is one baffling book!

ATLANTIC OCEAN
EUROPE
ITALY
AFRICA

FRANCE
SWITZ.
ITALY
Villa Mondragone
ALB.
Tyrrhenian Sea
Mediterranean Sea
Ionian Sea
TUNISIA

THE DETAILS

VOYNICH DISCOVERED the unintelligible tome while searching for valuable old books in an Italian monastery in Frascati, near Rome. Since that time, people have puzzled over and pondered the book's tattered yet colorful pages and rich, detailed illustrations, searching for answers. Today, the book lives under lock and key in a library at Yale University in New Haven, Connecticut, U.S.A.

THE CLUES

Even though Voynich died without being able to crack the code, there are some valuable clues we do know about this mysterious manuscript:

▶ **BAFFLING BOOK** The book was discovered in an old trunk from the Italian estate of Athanasius Kircher, a German priest and one of the most famous scholars of the 17th century.

▶ **A RIDDLE OF ABCs** Written in an unknown alphabet, the Voynich manuscript is 240 pages long.

▶ **ILLUSTRATION STATION** The manuscript contains unidentifiable, cartoonish botanical illustrations and drawings of stars, animals, and strange human figures.

THE THEORIES

SCHOLARS AND CRYPTOGRAPHERS—including a group of crack World War II code breakers—have studied the Voynich manuscript for more than a century, using a lot of grit, pencils, and computerized statistical analyses, but without much luck. In 2014, a British professor claimed to have deciphered 10 words of the tongue-twisting text, but others doubted his work. Some experts claim the manuscript contains an unknown language that has ties to the legendary artist Leonardo da Vinci. Other experts say it comes from Mexico and may be an ancient guide to herbal medicines or to alchemy. Unless someone makes a major breakthrough, we may never know the true story about this book—or what is written inside it.

(above) Is the Voynich manuscript the real-life da Vinci code? Famed Renaissance artist Leonardo da Vinci was known to sometimes write in a secret code and to even hide letters, numbers, and symbols in his paintings. Some people have speculated the Voynich manuscript code has links to the artist.

THIS BRAIN-BENDER STUMPS EVEN THE BEST CRYPTOLOGISTS.

THE BACKGROUND

A PUZZLING SCULPTURE named "Kryptos" sits in a courtyard on the grounds of the CIA headquarters in Langley, Virginia, U.S.A., not far from Washington, D.C. This coded artwork contains four messages, only three of which have been solved—despite the fact that it is literally located right outside the windows of some of the smartest code breakers in the world. The confounding fourth message has puzzled code breakers since the unveiling of the sculpture in 1990.

This sculpture—riddled with letters and numbers—has sparked international debate. Will the fourth message ever be solved?

VIRGINIA
UNITED STATES

OHIO | PA. | N.J.
W. VA. | MD. | DEL.
KY. | Langley | VIRGINIA
TENN. | NORTH CAROLINA | ATLANTIC OCEAN

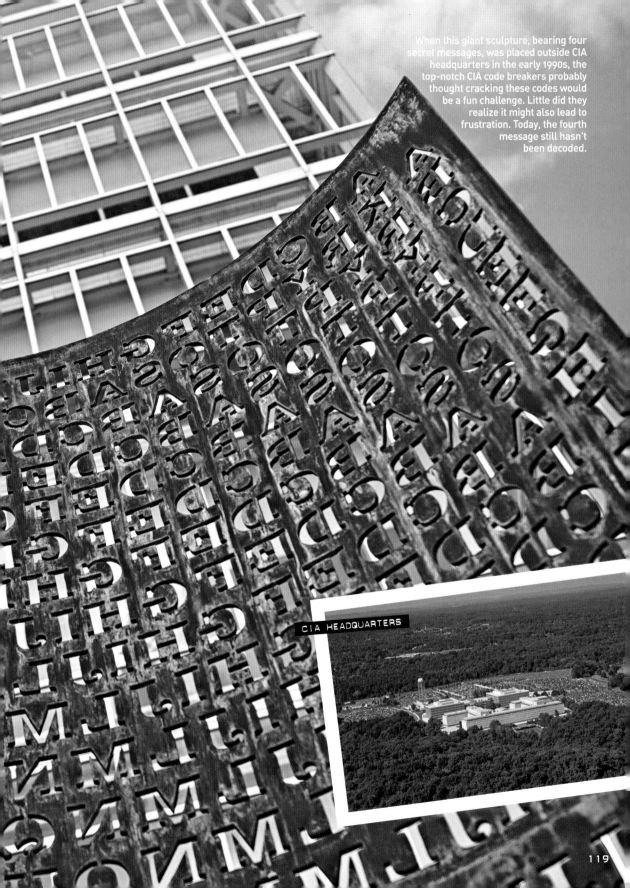

When this giant sculpture, bearing four secret messages, was placed outside CIA headquarters in the early 1990s, the top-notch CIA code breakers probably thought cracking these codes would be a fun challenge. Little did they realize it might also lead to frustration. Today, the fourth message still hasn't been decoded.

CIA HEADQUARTERS

JIM SANBORN

"KRYPTOS" means "hidden" in Greek and is the root of other words related to **CRYPTOLOGY.**

THE CLUES

Getting to the bottom of this intriguing mystery means learning more about it. What do you make of these clues?

> **TICKTOCK** So far, the artist who created the sculptural puzzle has dished on two words of the fourth message to help fans solve it. On the final panel (97 characters long), characters 64 to 74 spell "Berlin Clock."

> **THEMES AND MEMES** The three other puzzles on "Kryptos" that have been solved revealed passages or text from music and history.

> **HIDDEN MEANING** The sculpture was unveiled in November 1990, and experts say the month of November is a running theme in its message.

THE DETAILS

THE COPPER sculpture stands 12 feet (3.7 m) high and includes 865 punched out letters. The creator of this perplexing piece of art (a sculptor named Jim Sanborn, well-known for his science-based public works of art) has hinted that more clues to this mysterious puzzle might be found by studying the history of a famous clock in Europe, called the Berlin Clock, which intrigued Sanborn while he was working on his "Kryptos" sculpture.

BERLIN CLOCK

park inn

THE THEORIES

NEITHER CLUE PROVIDED by the puzzle's creator seems to have helped much when it comes to the tricky final panel. Some say solution seekers must first figure out the Berlin Clock itself. This clever clock "tells" time with a series of blinking and solid lights. Anyone wanting to know the time must observe patterns and calculate from there. On the other hand, some say Sanborn's "Berlin Clock" clue is a trick. They say the word "clock" might refer instead to a mathematical method developed in Poland. Will this final puzzle ever be solved? If only members of the public were allowed into CIA headquarters to give it a try!

WHAT DOES THE FOLLY SAY?

THE BACKGROUND

1 **SUFFERIN' CIPHERTEXT!** The meaning behind this stately series of letters engraved on an 18th-century monument has eluded scholars for centuries. Created more than 250 years ago by a Flemish sculptor, the monument itself sits under a rustic stone arch in a leafy garden at Shugborough Hall in Staffordshire, England. The letters on the monument are beautiful to look at, but for many years their meaning remained a mystery.

Get out your magnifying glass and check out what we know about this ancient and intriguing inscription.

THE DETAILS

2 **THE MONUMENT IS** a stone-and-marble folly. In architectural terms, the word "folly" refers to something created just for decoration. The rustic stone arch that frames the monument has two carved stone heads—a smiling,

SHUGBOROUGH HALL, in Staffordshire, England, might have a secret in its garden. What do the letters engraved in this beautiful stone arch mean?

SHUGBOROUGH HALL

bald man and a serious guy with little goat horns. No one knows who carved the mysterious letters below the relief (the part of the sculpture that shows a scene).

THE THEORIES

3 ONE LINGUISTICS EXPERT, American scientist Keith Massey, believes he's deciphered the Shugborough code. He says it means "Oro Ut Omnes Sequantur Viam Ad Veram Vitam," which translates from Latin to English as "I pray that all may follow the Way to True Life." Other theories include one that the curious sequence of letters is a clue, left by fanatical medieval knights, to the whereabouts of the missing Holy Grail, a highly sought-after Christian relic. Others think that the letters could just be for decoration.

NEW EVIDENCE REVEALED!

In 2011, a Scottish historian and expert in graves and monuments, A. J. Morton, revealed that he had solved the riddle of the Shugborough inscription. He said that the letters were not much more than early 19th-century graffiti left behind by former residents of the grand estate.

TREASURE TROVES

Home to mysterious lost gold and unsolved crimes, Arizona, U.S.A.'s parched Superstition Mountains—a vast and harsh desert wilderness not far from Phoenix—hides its secrets in endless barren canyons and desolate peaks. Native Americans established villages here between A.D. 800 and 1400. If you visit, you might see treasures like lizards, scorpions, and bear tracks, but you probably won't find lost gold!

YOU DON'T HAVE TO HAVE pirates' blood running through your veins to hunt for buried treasure or search for lost gold. But this time-tested get-rich-quick scheme isn't always as simple as X marks the spot. Sometimes loot is left in dangerous places, like on lonely islands, in the desert, or stuck in murky waterways. Lives have been lost searching for hidden treasure. Let's search for some of the most famous missing treasures ...

TREASURE LOOP
TRAIL NO. 56

THE SECRETS OF THIS
MUDDY
MYSTERY
MAY NEVER COME
CLEAN.

MEDIEVAL SILVER PENNY

The Fens—a low, marshy area in eastern England that's prone to flooding—made the perfect setting to the mysterious disappearance of King John's treasure.

THE BACKGROUND

THIS MYSTERY ROSE from the muck 800 years ago. In 1216, King John of England lost a large load of treasure at a river crossing. The loot quickly disappeared, never to be seen again. Many would say greedy King John got what he deserved when he lost his loot. Many of his subjects referred to the medieval monarch as "King John the Bad." He was known to be disloyal and dishonest, and he murdered many. King John never did find all his missing loot. But centuries later, people are still looking for his lost treasure. Could it still be stuck in the mud?

EUROPE
UNITED
KINGDOM
AFRICA
ATLANTIC
OCEAN
UNITED
KINGDOM   North
Sea
IRELAND
River Wellstream
FRANCE

The story of King John's
LOST TREASURE
has been handed down by word of mouth for
800 YEARS.

THE DETAILS

AT THE TIME King John lost his treasure, the tyrannical king was on the run from the threat of being overthrown. He would have been traveling with a convoy of carriages with a "baggage train" hauling the unlucky load of silver, gold, and the crown jewels. The baggage train—along with the men driving it and the horses pulling it—was lost in the rising tides at a murky crossing of the River Wellstream.

THE CLUES

So far all we know was that King John didn't want to share his loot. In his rush to get out of town, he lost it all. These clues might help us modern-day treasure hunters find it 800 years later.

PRICELESS King John's treasure included the king's regalia (the crown adorned with precious stones and other priceless bejeweled pieces).

SALTY Using special scanning and GPS data technology, researchers have discovered that the area King John would have crossed with his treasure would have been a salt marsh.

LONG LOST If any treasure still exists to be unearthed, it would be buried under centuries of silt, or fine sediment.

THIS DRAMATIC ILLUS-
TRATION SHOWS WHAT IT
MIGHT HAVE BEEN LIKE
WHEN KING JOHN AND HIS
MEN CROSSED THE FENS
AT HIGH TIDE.

THE THEORIES

SOME EXPERTS SAY King John's treasure was lost in the marsh because he was making a hasty escape across the river at high tide. He may not have had a good guide to keep him, or his stuff, safe. Because of shifting water and tides, the treasure is likely buried deep and far from the spot of the original crossing. Today, most of England's medieval marshes have been filled in and paved with roads or planted with crops. In this case, though, historians, archaeologists, and other treasure seekers have followed a trail of information provided by patterns in ancient tides and water drainage, aerial photographs, and GPS data throughout a very large area to try and locate the lost treasure. So far, though, no one's turned up this treasure.

LOST DUTCHMAN'S MINE

THIS SOUTHWEST QUEST MIGHT HOLD THE MOTHER LODE.

THE BACKGROUND

THE VAST AND BARREN DESERTS of Arizona's arid Superstition Mountains are home to century-old secrets and legends of gold, curses, killings, and fortunes lost and found. One legend has to do with a gold miner named Jacob Waltz, who found a fortune, kept it hidden, and died before giving anybody good directions on how to find it. Locating this loot will take a lot of luck. The mountain range where the mine is supposedly located stretches across 160,000 thirsty desert acres (647.5 sq km).

No one has ever solved Waltz's golden riddle of where to find the mine filled with his treasure. Care to give it a go?

UNITED STATES
ARIZONA

NEV. UTAH

Superstition Mountains

NEW MEXICO

CAL.

ARIZONA

U.S.
MEXICO

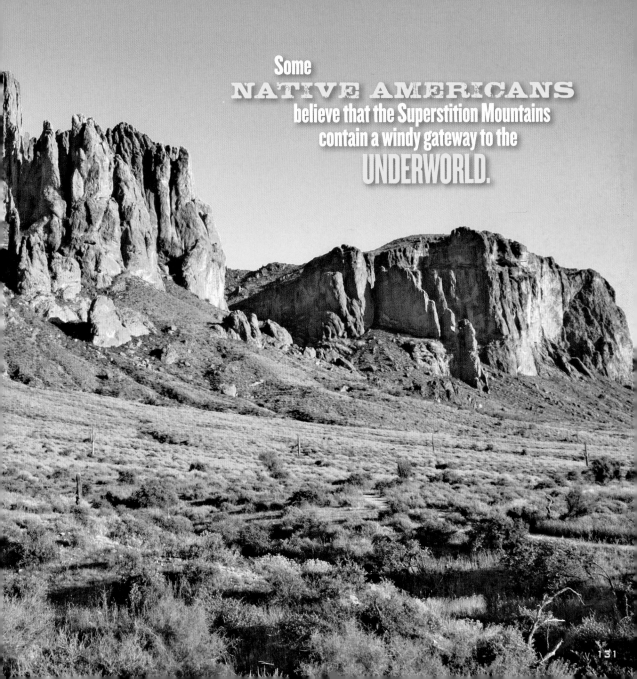

The base of Superstition Mountains in the Lost Dutchman State Park, in Arizona, U.S.A., where a miner supposedly found a fortune

Some **NATIVE AMERICANS** believe that the Superstition Mountains contain a windy gateway to the **UNDERWORLD.**

THE DETAILS

JACOB WALTZ was a German immigrant who said he had discovered a huge hoard of gold somewhere within Arizona's remote desert wilderness, home to snakes, spiders, cactus quills, and a lot of dust and rocks. People nicknamed the mysterious mine the "Lost Deutschman" or "Lost German" mine. On his deathbed in 1891, Waltz supposedly left clues for how to find his mine in the mountains, including a crude map. People have been searching for the treasure ever since.

GOLD NUGGETS IN THEIR NATURAL STATE

THE THEORIES

THE CLUES

Historians and treasure seekers think the contents of this treasure trove could be worth hundreds of millions of dollars. But so far, no one's found so much as a nugget.

▶ **MUDDLED MAP** Using landmarks like a heart, X marks, double circles, and arrows, Waltz created a mysterious map that he said would lead to his hidden treasure.

▶ **SOMEWHERE OUT THERE** Some reports say the mine is located northeast of an area now called Apache Junction.

▶ **MINE ALL MINE** Jacob Waltz once said his mine was located where no one would know to look.

MANY HAVE TRIED to follow the clues left by the German miner about how to find his mysterious mine. During his life, he is rumored to have killed people who had any idea of where it was. His scheme to keep things a secret seemed to work. After his death, nobody had a clue where the fortune was, despite the map he left behind, which only led to more questions than answers. One "Dutch hunter," Wayne Tuttle, has spent some 40 years looking for meaning behind the clues Waltz left. Others have spent money and time analyzing ore samples in the area for traces of gold that might lead to the prize.

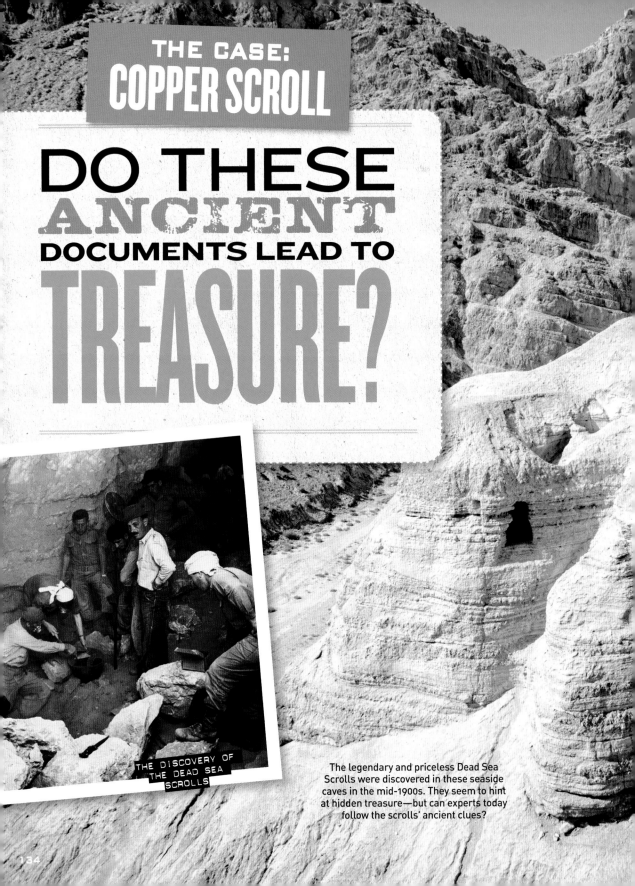

COPPER SCROLL

DO THESE ANCIENT DOCUMENTS LEAD TO TREASURE?

THE DISCOVERY OF THE DEAD SEA SCROLLS

The legendary and priceless Dead Sea Scrolls were discovered in these seaside caves in the mid-1900s. They seem to hint at hidden treasure—but can experts today follow the scrolls' ancient clues?

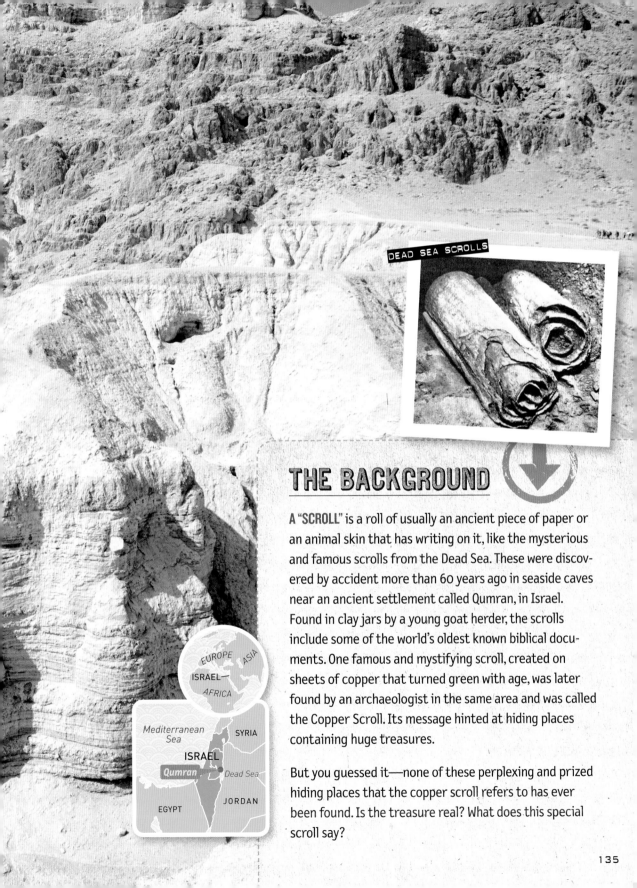

DEAD SEA SCROLLS

THE BACKGROUND

A "SCROLL" is a roll of usually an ancient piece of paper or an animal skin that has writing on it, like the mysterious and famous scrolls from the Dead Sea. These were discovered by accident more than 60 years ago in seaside caves near an ancient settlement called Qumran, in Israel. Found in clay jars by a young goat herder, the scrolls include some of the world's oldest known biblical documents. One famous and mystifying scroll, created on sheets of copper that turned green with age, was later found by an archaeologist in the same area and was called the Copper Scroll. Its message hinted at hiding places containing huge treasures.

But you guessed it—none of these perplexing and prized hiding places that the copper scroll refers to has ever been found. Is the treasure real? What does this special scroll say?

EUROPE ASIA

ISRAEL—

AFRICA

Mediterranean Sea

SYRIA

ISRAEL

Qumran

Dead Sea

JORDAN

EGYPT

The SCROLLS were written without **PUNCTUATION** making them hard to understand.

EXPERTS RESTORING DEAD SEA SCROLL FRAGMENTS

THE ISRAEL MUSEUM IN JERUSALEM, WHICH HOUSES THE DEAD SEA SCROLLS

THE DETAILS

THE TEXT ON THE COPPER SCROLL describes 67 hiding places where stores of gold, silver, copper, and other riches are hiding. But much of the scroll's messages are difficult to understand. Even though Hebrew is a known language, the text is filled with ancient vocabulary that's hard for modern linguists to decipher.

THE CLUES

Since its discovery, researchers have tried to piece together this puzzle. There's so much we do and don't know about the Copper Scroll:

▶ **HANDLE WITH CARE** The famous Copper Scroll was actually written on thin sheets of copper that were so brittle it took experts five years to open them without breaking them.

▶ **WEIGHTY WORDS** Text on the Copper Scroll refers to "the fortress which is in the Vale of Achor, forty cubits under the steps entering to the east" and "a money chest … of a weight of seventeen talents." A talent is a unit of weight and currency used by ancient Greeks and Romans.

▶ **LANDMARKS** The text on the Copper Scroll in one section refers to treasure hidden near a gutter. Another section refers to a reservoir.

THE THEORIES

MANY EXPERTS AGREE that the Copper Scroll—in the context of dark caves, biblical references, buried treasure, and secrets kept for thousands of years—sounds more like a prop for an adventure movie than a real relic from history. Some say the treasure, as described on the scroll, would be worth more than a million dollars. But the information provided by the scroll is sketchy. The names of places and landmarks in the areas referred to on the scroll—like one gutter or another—have also changed or disappeared over the millennia. Some experts simply dismiss the Copper Scroll's fantastical promises as pure fiction. But who knows, maybe the treasure is out there just waiting to be discovered!

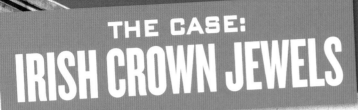

IRISH CROWN JEWELS

YOU'LL NEED THE LUCK OF THE IRISH TO SOLVE THIS GEM OF A WHODUNIT.

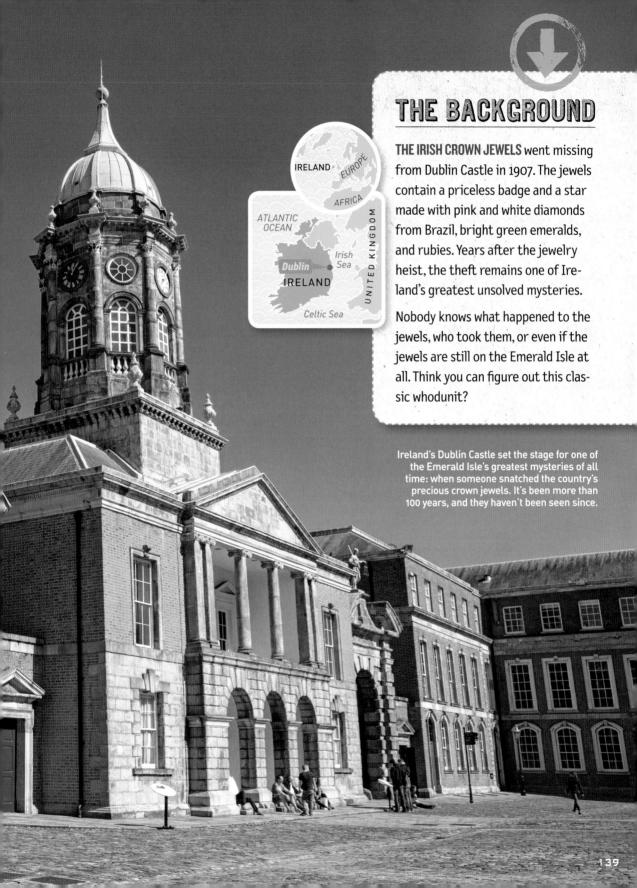

THE BACKGROUND

THE IRISH CROWN JEWELS went missing from Dublin Castle in 1907. The jewels contain a priceless badge and a star made with pink and white diamonds from Brazil, bright green emeralds, and rubies. Years after the jewelry heist, the theft remains one of Ireland's greatest unsolved mysteries.

Nobody knows what happened to the jewels, who took them, or even if the jewels are still on the Emerald Isle at all. Think you can figure out this classic whodunit?

Ireland's Dublin Castle set the stage for one of the Emerald Isle's greatest mysteries of all time: when someone snatched the country's precious crown jewels. It's been more than 100 years, and they haven't been seen since.

IRELAND
EUROPE
AFRICA

ATLANTIC OCEAN
Dublin
Irish Sea
IRELAND
Celtic Sea
UNITED KINGDOM

THE DETAILS

IN 1907, Ireland's priceless crown jewels had a market value of about $60,000, which would be the equivalent of more than a million dollars today. They had been kept in a bank vault, but at the time of the heist they had just been moved out of the vault into Dublin Castle for safekeeping. But the castle safe wasn't so safe.

THE CLUES

This sparkling mystery has kept a lot of people wondering exactly what happened to those precious, priceless jewels. Can we figure it out?

▶ **SLOW RESPONSE** Officials and guards didn't report the theft for more than a month. Why's that?

▶ **KEY TO THE MYSTERY** The safe at Dublin Castle was kept in the library. The keys were kept by Sir Arthur Vicars, a British knight. Was he involved?

▶ **IT WASN'T ME** Vicars was accused of failing to care for the regalia, but he blamed his second-in-command, Francis Shackleton, for the crime. After some inquiries, Shackleton was not found responsible.

The CROWN JEWELS were etched with the motto QUIS SEPARABIT? — which translates to "Who can separate us?"

Ireland is called the Emeral Isle thanks to its green landscape. But could actual gems be hidden somewhere in these hills?

THE THEORIES

THIS ROBBERY CREATED an international scandal worthy of legend, but there's no happy ending to this story, at least not yet. One royal inquiry noted that those in charge hadn't exercised "due vigilance or proper care" of the regalia (aka crown jewels), since they had made the decision to move the jewels out of the safety of their vault. In other words, those in charge hadn't done a good job keeping track of the goods. Were they careless or covering up a theft? Because the theft wasn't reported for more than a month, some people speculated it was an inside job. The hunt for the jewels came back to life in 1983, when detectives in Ireland got a credible tip about the jewels' whereabouts. Investigators undertook a huge search with dogs and metal detectors in the Dublin Mountains, but nothing came of the effort except for a lot more questions.

AN ARTIST'S DEPICTION OF WHAT THE IRISH CROWN JEWELS MIGHT LOOK LIKE

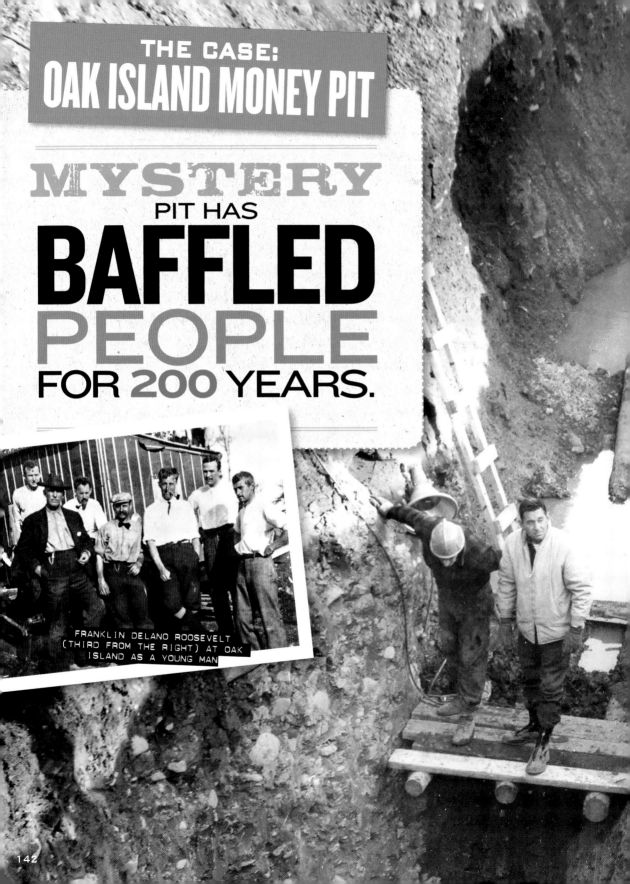

THE CASE:
OAK ISLAND MONEY PIT

MYSTERY PIT HAS BAFFLED PEOPLE FOR 200 YEARS.

FRANKLIN DELANO ROOSEVELT (THIRD FROM THE RIGHT) AT OAK ISLAND AS A YOUNG MAN

THE BACKGROUND

THE MYSTERY STARTED with a 16-year-old boy hunting on an uninhabited one-mile (1.6-km)-long island in Nova Scotia, Canada, in 1795. He noticed a depression in the ground and an old pulley from a ship hanging nearby in a tree. Thinking he'd discovered signs of buried treasure from a pirate ship, he and his friends dug and dug, discovering a strange man-made shaft but no treasure. They eventually gave up. But curiosity about the promising pit didn't end there. The initial dig inspired a frenzy that lasted for the next 200 years, revealing one new baffling piece of evidence after the next. Treasure hunters have schlepped, sweated, excavated, and drilled hundreds of feet into this seemingly bottomless pit on the remote Canadian island trying to find whatever it is that somebody went to a lot of trouble to bury.

CANADA
NOVA SCOTIA

NEW BRUNSWICK
P.E.I.
NOVA SCOTIA
Oak Island
ATLANTIC OCEAN

For more than 200 years, treasure seekers have invested time, money, and sweat into prospecting for buried valuables in what many call the "money pit" on Oak Island.

THE DETAILS

TREASURE SEEKERS have turned up in droves with sophisticated tools (and even camera crews) to document the depths of this mysterious pit. Some people have worked their way more than 100 feet (30.5 m) down. Others have discovered an elaborate system of drains built inside the pit. Despite all the searching, no one has found the big treasure yet.

THE CLUES

During all the years of digging, people have found some seriously strange stuff in the pit.

▶ **WATERLOGGED** Every 10 feet (3 m) down, the pit has a floor made of oak logs.

▶ **STRANGE STUFF** A tiny bit of treasure has been found in the pit: bits of gold chain and a scrap of old parchment paper with the letters "vi" written on it with a quill pen and loads of coconut fiber. But coconuts aren't native to Canada.

▶ **TRAPPED** A sophisticated trap guards whatever is buried in this famous pit. Excavators in 1850 triggered the trap, which flooded the pit, making the quest even harder.

A FAMILY OF EXCAVATORS ON OAK ISLAND IN 1963

THE THEORIES

PEOPLE OVER THE YEARS have attempted to explain what's going on under the sand and dirt of this mysterious island. Theories relating to this island mystery span from Shakespeare's missing manuscript, to long-hidden pirate treasure, but so far excursions into the pit have only added up to millions of dollars, multiple deaths, and more questions than answers. Over the centuries, there are legends of curses and stories about packs of dogs guarding the treasure.

Some say rare Egyptian treasure is hiding in the depths. Others wonder if it is an elaborate burial ground. Or if it could be a hiding place for the bounty belonging to a famous pirate like Captain Kidd or Blackbeard. Others say the French crown jewels might have been hidden there during the French Revolution. Treasure buffs, scientists, and scholars continue to dig for answers to this bottomless pit of a puzzle.

Franklin Delano **ROOSEVELT** was among those who came to find **FORTUNE** on Oak Island as a young man.

EASTER EGG HUNT WORTH
MILLIONS!

ALEXANDER III of Russia commissioned jeweler Peter Carl Fabergé to create elaborate eggs crafted out of gold and jewels. Some 50 were made, but only 43 have been found. So where are the rest?

THE BACKGROUND

1 **FOR MORE THAN A CENTURY,** Fabergé Easter eggs have been prized possessions of the very rich and the royal. Crafted in the shops of Peter Carl Fabergé from 1885 to 1917, most of these priceless, unique, and glitzy eggs were designed at the request of Russian tsars Alexander III and Nicholas II (that was Anastasia's father, from page 46) as glittering Easter gifts for their families. One of the most sparkling examples is the Winter Egg, which is studded with 3,000 diamonds and sold at a 2004 auction for $9.6 million. Fabergé allegedly made 50 imperial eggs in all.

Although 43 of the eggs are safely nested in museums or private collections around the world, seven of them are mysteriously missing. Are they sitting snugly in bank vaults somewhere in the world? Their whereabouts remain an eggs-citing mystery to this day.

THE FABERGÉ
Imperial Coronation Egg, estimated to be worth
$18 to $24 million

THE DETAILS

2 **EXPERTS BELIEVE** the Fabergé eggs that were so coveted by the Russian royal family symbolized the greed and crookedness that eventually led to political upheaval in 1917. When Peter Carl Fabergé closed up shop in St. Petersburg, Russia, that year, no imperial eggs were ever made again. The eggs were eventually sold off after the execution of the royal family, but only 43 were recovered, mostly within the borders of Russia.

THE THEORIES

3 **SOME EXPERTS SAY** the missing eggs may have been destroyed during the Russian Revolution. Others say they could be sitting around people's homes, unidentified.

NEW EVIDENCE REVEALED!

In 2014, an American scrap metal dealer bought what he thought was a tacky knickknack at a flea market. On a whim he searched for information about its markings and realized it was the third imperial egg, made in 1887. It was worth almost $38 million! But that could mean the seven missing eggs are still out there somewhere, so keep an eye out to help "crack" the case!

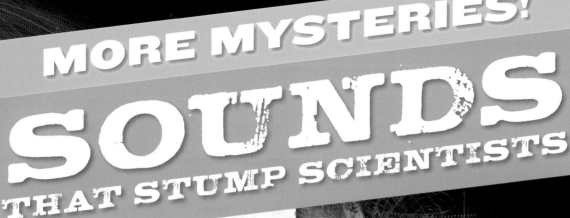

SOUNDS
THAT STUMP SCIENTISTS

WHAT WAS THAT NOISE? Certain sounds have stumped scientists for centuries—whistles, rattles, hums, and mysterious space music. What does it all mean? Are these noises explainable through science? Are they the sound of tectonic plates shifting? Or are they maybe, a bit, out of this world? Turn up the volume, let the sound waves ripple right into your brain, and check out these seriously strange sounds to see what you think.

A HYDROPHONE IS A KIND OF MICROPHONE DESIGNED TO LISTEN TO AND RECORD UNDERWATER SOUND.

THE BLOOP

THIS SOUND SOUNDS LIKE a combination between a giant lawn mower and a belch. It's one of the loudest sounds—if not the loudest—ever recorded in the ocean. In the summer of 1997, this hiccup was heard repeatedly across the Pacific Ocean from 3,100 miles (5,000 km) away. It was heard by scientists listening to ocean sounds through hydrophones in the Scotia Sea, which is part of the South Atlantic Ocean. But not even a blue whale could make a noise that loud. So what made all that racket? It's a mystery. Around the time it was first documented, some experts suggested that the bloop was the sound of a massive unknown, deep-sea creature. But the U.S. National Oceanic and Atmospheric Administration says the bloop wasn't an animal but rather the cracking of an ice shelf or an "ice quake."

TAOS HUM

IN THE 1990S, when people in the small town of Taos, New Mexico, U.S.A., started reporting a mysterious humming noise, the phenomenon made national news. Some said the sound woke them up at night. Others said the noise rattled their teeth. It sounded like a big truck idling or a giant refrigerator ... well, refrigerating. Despite scientific measurements of seismic and electromagnetic vibrations in the area, the sound remains a mystery. Some speculated it came from great underground engines that powered secret military installations, a buried spaceship, magma moving around under the crust of the Earth, or maybe just the desert wind. In the 1990s, retired physicist Joe Mullins led a group of scientists who interviewed "hum hearers" and examined possible sources of the sound. He believes the hum is a worldwide thing that's been reported from Asia to Indiana, U.S.A. At the time, his task force concluded that people hearing the hum were affected by an ear disorder that causes a ringing in the ears. Another theory about the hum is that it was heard only by people who have unusually sharp hearing or were experiencing some kind of delusion. Scientists are keeping their ears to the ground to solve this mind-blowing mystery.

TAOS, NEW MEXICO

FLUTE SOUNDS

THIS MYSTERIOUS SOUND has residents of one Oregon, U.S.A., neighborhood in a real pickle. They say it whines, hisses, toots, and whistles. Is someone out there playing an eerie giant flute? Is a giant UFO hovering in the night sky? Are there ghosts in the woods practicing the piccolo? People have heard the noise at random times—day and night, lasting from a few seconds to a few minutes. Nobody seems to be able to explain it. Whatever it is, the freaky noise has kept the residents of Forest Grove, Oregon, on edge. Law enforcement and utility companies in the town investigated, but so far, no one's found the source of the sound.

MOON SOUNDS

IN 1969, while orbiting the far side of the moon and out of broadcast range of the Earth, Apollo 10 astronauts puzzled over mysterious music they heard, remarking that the unnerving noise sounded "outer-spacey." Nobody really knows what the sounds were, or where they came from. Maybe the sounds were something easy to explain, like screaming aliens. But they didn't hear anything this superspooky the other 30 times the lunar module orbited the moon on that mission. One NASA technician says the freaky noises had nothing to do with aliens but rather with radio interference between the lunar module and the command module. This makes sense given that sound cannot travel through space because sound waves require a medium, such as air or water, to travel through.

SOLVING MYSTERIES:

AN
INTERVIEW
WITH
CHRIS FISHER

SINCE HE WAS A KID, Chris Fisher has been fascinated with what people can learn from investigating and reconstructing history. Today, as an archaeologist and a National Geographic Explorer, he studies lost civilizations in countries from the United States to Honduras to Albania. Here, Fisher shares some of his thoughts about what we can learn from exploring history's mysteries:

THE FUTURE As an archaeologist, I'm always trying to imagine what a place used to look like and how people lived. It's fun to discover old objects and try to understand why and how they got where they ended up. But archaeology

BOWL ARTIFACT UNCOVERED AT THE WHITE CITY

is not just about finding objects, it's about learning from the objects. We try to piece together how past people assembled themselves. Then we can learn from them to solve today's problems and build a better future.

FIELD DAY
Out in the field, like in Honduras at the site of the White City of the Jaguar, it's fun to wake up every morning with the howler monkeys before dawn. As an archaeologist, I get to enjoy the outdoors a lot, like hiking and discovering wildlife and plants. Archaeology is a very hands-on job. If we're excavating, I carry a mason's trowel and a notebook. If I'm walking around doing a survey, I'll have a GPS unit in one hand and a machete in the other hand to cut down tall grass. I also use the machete to pick things up so I don't get bitten by a snake.

DIRT
Some archaeologists go into an excavation and come out looking like they haven't ever been outside. But that's not me. I'm usually covered in dirt as soon as I get out of the car. It's a constant struggle

ANIMAL FIGURE UNCOVERED AT THE WHITE CITY

to stay clean. If we're camping, like in the Mosquitia region in eastern Honduras, it might be five or six days before I can take a shower or wash my clothes.

FANTASTIC FEATHERS
One of the most amazing artifacts I ever found at the White City of the Jaguar was the centerpiece of a cache of priceless objects. The artifact was a statue of a bird wearing something like a harness. Some archaeologists believe it represents a vulture. But I think it was a parrot or a resplendent quetzal. At the time, these birds were highly revered. Their iridescent feathers (and the birds) were some of the most valuable items you could own in prehistoric America.

YOU CAN TOO!
If you want to be an archaeologist one day, learn another language. The better you can speak another language, like Spanish, the better off you'll be when you're working in another country. Learning to write is also important. Sharing what you learn is one of the most important parts of an archaeologist's job.

CHRIS FISHER (CENTER) ON SITE AT THE WHITE CITY OF THE JAGUAR

AFTERWORD

IT'S NO JOKE—real life can be stranger than fiction! Have you ever had any mystifying, eerie, or spine-tingling encounters you just can't explain? Who knows, there could be hidden treasure, evidence of lost civilizations, or even dinosaur bones buried just below your feet right now. Imagine all the mysteries still out there waiting to be uncovered or solved. Embrace your inner sleuth and keep your eyes open—you never know what you might discover!

INDEX

INDEX

INDEX

ILLUSTRATION CREDITS

CREDITS

For kids all over the world who follow their curiosity and never stop asking questions —KJ

Since 1888, the National Geographic Society has funded more than 12,000 research, exploration, and preservation projects around the world. The Society receives funds from National Geographic Partners, LLC, funded in part by your purchase. A portion of the proceeds from this book supports this vital work. To learn more, visit natgeo.com/info.

For more information, visit national geographic.com, call 1-800-647-5463, or write to the following address:

National Geographic Partners
1145 17th Street N.W.
Washington, D.C. 20036-4688 U.S.A.

Visit us online at nationalgeographic.com/books

For librarians and teachers:
ngchildrensbooks.org

More for kids from National Geographic:
kids.nationalgeographic.com

For information about special discounts for bulk purchases, please contact National Geographic Books Special Sales: specialsales@natgeo.com

For rights or permissions inquiries, please contact National Geographic Books Subsidiary Rights: bookrights@natgeo.com

Art directed by Kathryn Robbins
Designed by James Hiscott, Jr.

The publisher would like to thank everyone who made this book possible: Ariane Szu-Tu, editor; Sarah J. Mock, senior photo editor; Anne LeongSon and Gus Tello, design production assistants; Sally Abbey, managing editor; and Joan Gossett, editorial production manager.

Trade paperback ISBN: 978-1-4263-2871-8

Reinforced library binding ISBN: 978-1-4263-2872-5

Printed in Hong Kong
17/THK/1